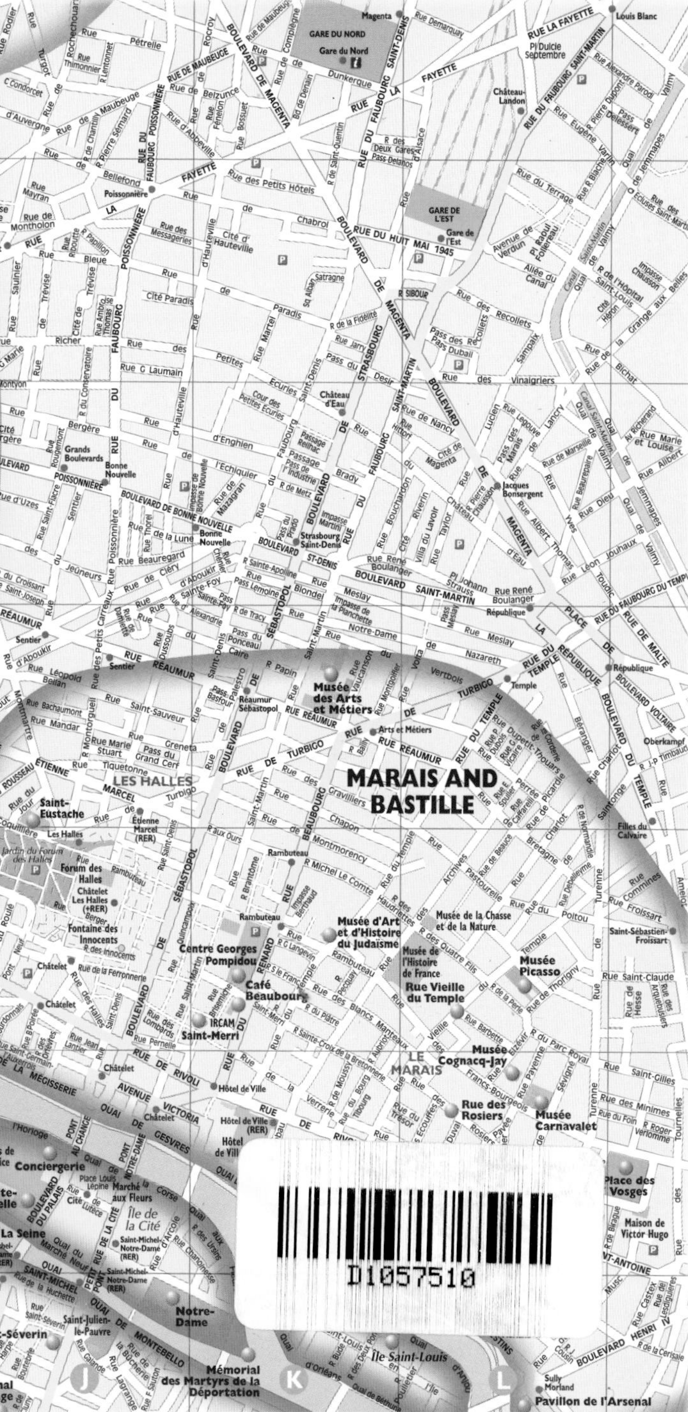

MARAIS AND BASTILLE
GARE DU NORD
Gare du Nord
Magenta
Louis Blanc
Pl Dulcie Septembre
Château-Landon
Poissonnière
GARE DE L'EST
Gare de l'Est
RUE DU HUIT MAI 1945
Château d'Eau
Grands Boulevards
Bonne Nouvelle
Strasbourg Saint-Denis
Jacques Bonsergent
République
Sentier
Réaumur Sébastopol
Musée des Arts et Métiers
Arts et Métiers
Temple
Oberkampf
LES HALLES
Saint-Eustache
Les Halles
Étienne Marcel (RER)
Jardin du Forum des Halles
Forum des Halles
Châtelet Les Halles (+RER)
Fontaine des Innocents
Rambuteau
Filles du Calvaire
Musée d'Art et d'Histoire du Judaïsme
Musée de la Chasse et de la Nature
Saint-Sébastien-Froissart
Musée de l'Histoire de France
Centre Georges Pompidou
Café Beaubourg
Rue Vieille du Temple
Musée Picasso
Châtelet
IRCAM
Saint-Merri
LE MARAIS
Musée Cognacq-Jay
Hôtel de Ville
Hôtel de Ville (RER)
Rue des Rosiers
Musée Carnavalet
Conciergerie
Marché aux Fleurs
Île de la Cité
Cité
Place des Vosges
Maison de Victor Hugo
La Seine
Saint-Michel-Notre-Dame (RER)
Notre-Dame
Saint-Julien-le-Pauvre
Mémorial des Martyrs de la Déportation
Île Saint-Louis
Sully Morland
Pavillon de l'Arsenal
BOULEVARD DE MAGENTA
RUE LA FAYETTE
BOULEVARD DE SÉBASTOPOL
BOULEVARD SAINT-MARTIN
PLACE DE LA RÉPUBLIQUE
RUE DE RIVOLI
QUAI DE GESVRES
BOULEVARD HENRI IV
J
K
L

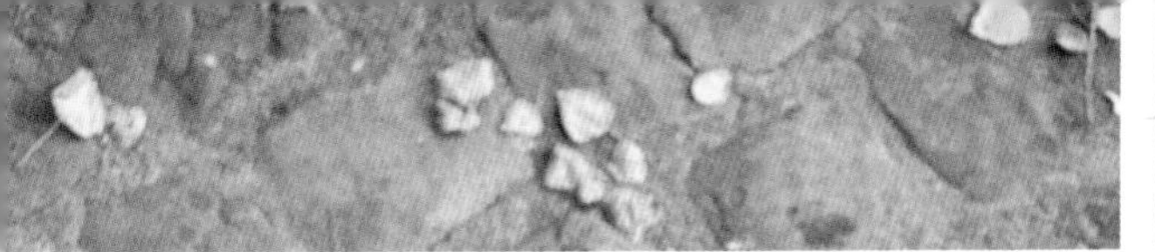

CITYPACK TOP 25
Paris

FIONA DUNLOP
ADDITIONAL WRITING BY HEIDI ELLISON

AA Publishing
If you have any comments or suggestions for this guide you can contact the editor at *travelguides@TheAA.com*

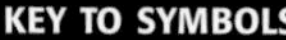

How to Use This Book

KEY TO SYMBOLS

- Map reference to the accompanying fold-out map
- Address
- Telephone number
- Opening/closing times
- Restaurant or café
- Nearest rail station
- Nearest Métro (subway) station
- Nearest bus route
- Nearest riverboat or ferry stop
- Facilities for visitors with disabilities
- Other practical information
- Further information
- Tourist information
- Admission charges: Expensive (over €10), Moderate (€4–€10) and Inexpensive (under €4)
- Major Sight ★ Minor Sight
- Walks
- Excursions
- Shops
- Entertainment and Nightlife
- Restaurants

This guide is divided into four sections

• Essential Paris: An introduction to the city and tips on making the most of your stay.

• Paris by Area: We've broken the city into six areas, and recommended the best sights, shops, entertainment venues, nightlife and restaurants in each one. Suggested walks help you to explore on foot.

• Where to Stay: The best hotels, whether you're looking for luxury, budget or something in between.

• Need to Know: The info you need to make your trip run smoothly, including getting about by public transport, weather tips, emergency phone numbers and useful websites.

Navigation In the Paris by Area chapter, we've given each area of the city its own colour, which is also used on the locator maps throughout the book and the map on the inside front cover.

Maps The fold-out map accompanying this book is a comprehensive street plan of Paris. The grid on this fold-out map is the same as the grid on the locator maps within the book. We've given grid references within the book for each sight and listing.

Contents

Introducing Paris

The City of Light needs no introduction: the Eiffel Tower, Sacré-Cœur, the Louvre. It is not a museum, however, but a vibrant urban area. The monuments won't change, but everything else will. Forget stereotypes and see the city with new eyes.

Paris has been making a concerted effort to change its image as a cold city full of rude, arrogant people. That reputation was never entirely deserved, but the good news for both visitors and residents is that Paris has undergone many changes for the better. The mayor's office and the national government sponsor a number of popular (and free) annual events along the lines of the *Fête de la Musique* (21 June), which bring the normally reserved Parisians out to have fun.

In addition to Paris Plage, when the Right Bank of the Seine becomes a sandy beach for one month in the summer, the city is the site of *La Nuit des Musées* (May), when several museums stay open all night; *Les Journées du Patrimoine* (September), when normally off-limits monuments are open, *La Nuit Blanche* (October), with all-night art and cultural events; and outdoor film festivals in the summer.

And Paris is no longer deserted in August. Once transformed into a quiet village while the entire working population holidayed elsewhere, the city has come back to life as the French learn to stagger their holidays. It's still quiet, but more and more restaurants and shops are open. Picnicking in the city is now popular and the banks of the Seine and parks are full of outdoor diners. The once-forbidden lawns in its parks and squares are covered with sunbathers and children.

Most visitors come to see the great monuments, however. Having miraculously survived wars and revolution—some of them for a thousand years—they now seem to be eternal.

Facts + Figures

Population: 2.2 million
Area: 105sq km (40.5sq miles)
GDP (Île de France): €534 billion
Highest elevation: Montmartre at 130m (423ft)
Mayor: Bertrand Delanoë (Socialist)
Divided into 20 *arrondissements*

FLIGHT OF FANCY

The first manned flight took place in Paris when Pilatre de Rozier and the Marquis d'Arlandes made a 25-minute trip in a hot-air balloon from the Bois de Boulogne to what is now the 13th *arrondissement* on 21 November 1783. Among the crowd observing their feat was none other than Benjamin Franklin, one of the founding fathers of the US.

CLOSED!

Every Tuesday a crowd of disappointed tourists gathers outside the closed entrance to the Louvre pyramid. Remember that most major museums are closed one day a week: Monday for the city-run museums (such as Musée Carnavalet and Musée d'Art Moderne de la Ville de Paris) and Tuesday for national museums (including the Louvre, Centre Pompidou and Grand Palais).

DID YOU KNOW?

- Every evening, nearly 300 Parisian monuments, hotels, churches, fountains, bridges and canals are illuminated against the night sky.
- France has finally banned smoking inside restaurants, bars and cafés, for the dining pleasure of all.
- Watch your step! In spite of the city's best efforts to alleviate the problem, dog droppings are still a hazard.

A Short Stay in Paris

DAY 1

Morning The *bateaux mouches* may be a cliché but they are a great way to get your bearings. From your floating seat on the **Seine** (▷ 48–49), you'll see most of the major monuments, from the **Eiffel Tower** (▷ 30–31) and the **Musée d'Orsay** (▷ 26–27) to the **Louvre** (▷ 76–77) and Hôtel de Ville, while the commentary will give you some historical background.

Mid-morning When the one-hour trip ends, walk across the street from the square du Vert-Galant and through the place Dauphine, a hidden square where Yves Montand and his wife Simone Signoret once lived.

Lunch Return to the Pont Neuf, walk north towards the Right Bank and turn left onto the quai du Louvre, then right into the Louvre's Cour Carrée. Admire the building's sculpted facade as you walk through to the Cour Napoleon, site of I. M. Pei's famous glass pyramid, which you can further appreciate while lunching on the terrace of the **Café Marly** (▷ 86).

Afternoon Spend the afternoon in the **Louvre**, either concentrating on a preferred era or just wandering aimlessly. When (or if) you have had your fill of the treasures in the museum, the adjoining Carrousel du Louvre is full of boutiques of all descriptions.

Dinner Walk across the Pont du Carrousel, turn left on the quai Voltaire, right on the rue des Saints-Pères, left on the rue Jacob and right on the rue Saint-Benoît. Have dinner at **Le Petit Saint-Benoît** (▷ 56) for a taste of Old Paris at bargain prices.

Evening If you are still feeling energetic, you might want to take in a jazz concert at the **Caveau de la Huchette** (▷ 55) after dinner.

DAY 2

Morning Get an early start at the **Musée d'Orsay** (▷ 26–27), which opens at 9.30. Take your time visiting this vast former train station full of treasures of 19th-century art, concentrating on its rich collection of works by the great Impressionists, but without neglecting the decorative arts and sculpture sections.

Lunch On leaving the museum, turn left on the quai Anatole France and continue on the quai d'Orsay until you reach the rue Malar and turn left again (or take the RER from the Musée d'Orsay station to Pont de l'Alma). Sample specialities from the Basque region at **L'Ami Jean** (▷ 36), famed for its mashed potatoes *(purée)* and meat-and-fish combinations.

Afternoon Walk east on the rue de l'Université, admiring the handsome buildings and exclusive boutiques. You can spend the rest of the afternoon window-shopping. If you are keen on finding museum-quality antiques, you should turn left on the rue de Beaune, right on the quai Voltaire, right on the rue des Saints-Pères and right again on the rue de l'Université, completing the square. The streets in between are worth exploring as well. If you are more interested in fashion you should investigate the boutiques around Saint-Germain-des-Prés and Saint-Sulpice and continue up the rue du Cherche Midi.

Dinner Have dinner at **Thoumieux** (▷ 36) to soak up the lively brasserie atmosphere and sample the cassoulet, a bean-and-sausage stew that is a speciality of southwest France.

Evening Take an elevator ride to the upper floor of the **Eiffel Tower** (▷ 30–31) to see the City of Light glowing below while the tower glitters around you (on the hour for 10 minutes).

Top 25

Arc de Triomphe ▷ **74**
Monument to Napoleon's military might.

Centre Georges Pompidou ▷ **60–61**
Paris's wackiest building.

Conciergerie ▷ **40–41**
Marie-Antoinette's last home.

Versailles ▷ **103**
Louis XIV's magnificent palace, outside Paris.

Tour Eiffel ▷ **30–31**
The symbol of Paris, best at night.

La Seine boat trip
▷ **48–49** See the sights as you glide along the Seine.

Sainte-Chapelle
▷ **46–47** A jewel of a 13th-century royal chapel.

Sacré-Cœur ▷ **90–91**
A church perched on the city's highest point.

Place des Vosges ▷ **63**
Paris's most beautiful square.

Place de la Concorde
▷ **80** This square is superb at sunset.

Père Lachaise ▷ **102**
Some of your heroes may be buried here.

Palais de Chaillot ▷ **32**
Maritime and architecture museums and great views.

Opéra Palais Garnier
▷ **78** Extravagant Second Empire opera house.

These pages are a quick guide to the Top 25, which are described in more detail later. Here they are listed alphabetically and the tinted background shows the area they are in.

Galeries Vivienne and Colbert ▷ 75 Elegant 19th-century malls.

Les Invalides ▷ 24–25 May Napoleon rest in peace.

Jardin du Luxembourg ▷ 42 This stately park has something for everyone.

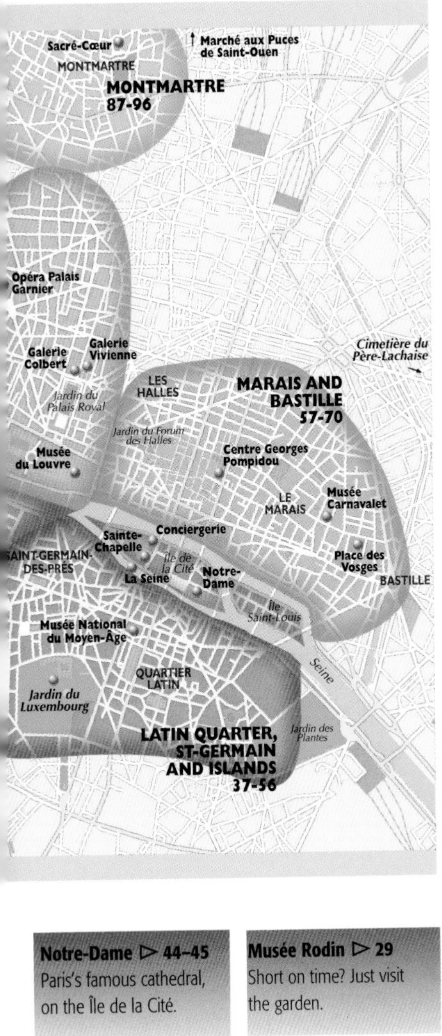

Marché aux Puces de Saint-Ouen ▷ 100 Antiques, furniture, clothing and just plain junk.

Musée Carnavalet ▷ 62 Discover Paris's turbulent past at this lively museum.

Musée du Louvre ▷ 76–77 A great museum, getting better all the time.

Musée Marmottan Monet ▷ 101 The world's largest collection of Monet's paintings and works by his contemporaries.

Musée National du Moyen-Âge ▷ 43 Don't miss the Unicorn tapestries in this Gothic mansion.

Musée d'Orsay ▷ 26–27 Heaven for lovers of Impressionism, in a converted train station.

Notre-Dame ▷ 44–45 Paris's famous cathedral, on the Île de la Cité.

Musée Rodin ▷ 29 Short on time? Just visit the garden.

Musée du quai Branly ▷ 28 Art from Asia, Africa, Oceania and the Americas.

Shopping

When it comes to shopping, Paris has it all: fine department stores, quirky and super-chic boutiques, inexpensive chain stores, big and small flea markets and everything in between.

Designer Fashions and Food

Narrow rue du Faubourg Saint-Honoré has the classiest shopping in the city, with Gucci, Versace, Hermès and Karl Lagerfeld, and several other top fashion names almost next door to each other. Prices are high but it certainly deserves a lingering window-shop if nothing else. It ends at rue Royale and place de la Madeleine, ringed by the greatest of Parisian food shops. There are many specialists in truffles, handmade chocolates and caviar, and the queen of all food halls, Fauchon.

Visitors from all over the country crowd into this area in search of the latest designer fashions and the fine foods. It's only a few minutes to boulevard Haussmann and the city's two stylish principal Belle Époque department stores, Galeries Lafayette and Printemps, complete with English-speaking hostesses.

Out of the Rain

Near the Pompidou Centre is the old Halles marketplace, now a popular indoor shopping area. In the Sentier and Opéra districts, just north, explore delightful covered alleys and shop-lined 19th-century *galeries*, which are an excellent place to linger if the weather is poor.

GOURMET PICNICS

There isn't a word for delicatessen in French. A *charcuterie* is a pork butcher and a *traiteur* a caterer, or a shop selling ready-cooked dishes. The two are closely related and are often combined. Inside, glass cabinets or counters display dozens of exquisite freshly prepared salads, grated carrots, paper-thin slices of cucumber, aubergines (eggplant), mushrooms, meat pies and spicy sausages, as well as garlic, bean-and-pork stew and a gourmet mix of cooked meats.

Shoppers have no shortage of choice in Paris, whether they're looking for high fashion or gourmet food

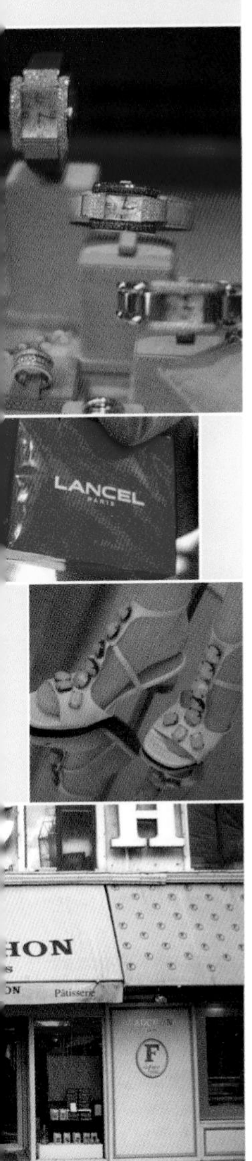

Left Bank Chic

Nip across the Seine, by Métro or on foot, to Saint-Germain-des-Prés. The grown-up part of the Left Bank is the place for antiquarian bookshops, antiques dealers, art galleries and, farther south, the city's oldest department store, Le Bon Marché, at 24 rue des Sèvres, with its food hall, La Grande Epicerie.

Buy the Best

In Paris look for French flair and quality, not bargains. Think not only fashion, lingerie and perfume, but high-quality cookware such as Le Creuset, superb knives by Sabatier, wonderful copper pans for making sauces, and kitchen gadgets such as perfect openers for champagne bottles and whisks that really work. Think also of stylish children's and baby clothes, plus, of course, prepared foods including *coq au vin* and pâtés, and unusual wines.

A Piece of Paris

If it's souvenirs of Paris you want you will find no shortage of cheap replicas of the Eiffel Tower, especially from sellers beneath the tower. You'll find better versions as paperweights in the specialist shops. Or bring home a Peugeot peppermill, a fine piece of kitchen engineering, or visit the galleries such as the Louvre, Musée d'Orsay and Musée Marmottan for postcards of the *Mona Lisa*, prints by Monet and posters of the Folies Bergères by Henri de Toulouse-Lautrec.

WHAT'S WHAT

Boulangeries sell baguettes, and more besides; try the *ficelle*, a thinner, finer loaf, or *pain au levain*, delicious sourdough bread. And then there are the croissants, *ordinaire* or *au beurre* (with butter). *Pâtisseries* sell pastries and tarts. *Charcuteries* sell cold meats, snails, cheese, truffles, wines, caviar and more. *Parfumeries* can stock solely French perfume but some sell cosmetics and soaps, too. *Bouquinistes* sell used books and prints, posters and postcards.

Shopping by Theme

Whether you're looking for a department store, a quirky boutique, or something in between, you'll find it all in Paris. On this page shops are listed by theme. For a more detailed write-up, see the individual listings in Paris by Area.

ACCESSORIES/SHOES

Iki Mezura (▷ 84)
Lollipops (▷ 54)
Louis Vuitton (▷ 84)

ANTIQUES

Galerie Captier (▷ 35)
Louvre des Antiquaires (▷ 84)

ART

Artazart (▷ 68)
Chalcographie du Louvre (▷ 84)

BEAUTY

Detaille (▷ 94)

BOOKS AND CDs

Galerie de l'Opéra de Paris (▷ 84)
La Hune (▷ 54)
Librairie des Abbesses (▷ 94)
Shakespeare and Company (▷ 54)

CANDLES AND SCENTS

Dyptique (▷ 54)

CLOTHES AND HATS

Agnès B (▷ 68)
Antik Batik (▷ 68)
Azzedine Alaïa (▷ 68)
Base One (▷ 94)
Chanel (▷ 84)
Colette (▷ 84)
Didier Ludot (▷ 84)
Judith Lacroix (▷ 94)
Kamille (▷ 94)
Marie Mercié (▷ 54)
Petit Bateau (▷ 94)
Sonia Rykiel (▷ 54)
Vanessa Bruno (▷ 68)

DEPARTMENT STORES

BHV (▷ 68)
Le Bon Marché Rive Gauche (▷ 35)
Galeries Lafayette (▷ 84, panel)
Printemps (▷ 84, panel)

FOOD AND DRINK

À la Mère de Famille (▷ 84)
Boulangerie Delmontel (▷ 94)
Charcuterie Lyonnaise (▷ 94)
Mariage Frères (▷ 54, 68)
Oliviers & Co (▷ 68)
Pierre Hermé (▷ 54)
Rue Mouffetard (▷ 54)

HOMES AND GARDENS

The Conran Shop (▷ 35)
Dehellerin (▷ 68)
La Droguerie (▷ 68)

MALLS

Forum des Halles (▷ 68)

MARKETS

Marché Barbès (▷ 94)
Marché aux Fleurs (▷ 54)
Marché de la rue Lepic (▷ 94)
Marché de la rue Montorgueil (▷ 68)

POSTERS

Galerie Documents (▷ 54)

TOYS

Si Tu Veux (▷ 84)

Paris by Night

Entertainment options range from in-line skating and clubbing to classical music or the Moulin Rouge

The heart of Paris has a special beauty at night, and an electric atmosphere. Boulevards, great monuments and historic buildings are dazzlingly illuminated. The Champs-Élysées, place de la Concorde and the Louvre make a magnificent spectacle of lights against the night sky. The soaring Eiffel Tower, shining like gold, and the silvery white of the Sacré-Cœur Basilica are majestic landmarks.

Glamorous Fun

There's a sense of excitement, anticipation and enjoyment. In addition to glamorous cabarets, there are the world-class ballet, concert and opera venues, nightclubs, discos, café-theatres and atmospheric bars with live music. Although the Métro is closed from 12.45am (1.45 Friday and Saturday) to 5.45am, many taxis run at night, as well as the Noctilien buses.

Added Magic

A boat trip along the Seine between the illuminated buildings adds extra magic—*bateaux mouches* run every evening until 11 (9 in winter). For experienced in-line skaters a high-speed three-hour skating tour of Paris takes place every Friday at 10pm (see www.pari-roller.com for details). Unless you are looking for the city's sleaziest clubs and revues, avoid the boulevard de Clichy and place Pigalle at the foot of Montmartre.

AN EVENING STROLL

Start at Châtelet and walk towards the Louvre along the embankment opposite the illuminated Conciergerie, the Monnaie and the Institut de France. At the Louvre make a detour into the magnificently lit Cour Carrée. Return to the river, cross the Pont des Arts, then walk back along the opposite bank, with views north of the stately Samaritaine and the Palais de Justice on the Île de la Cité. Continue towards Saint-Michel, then cross over to Notre Dame and make your way around the north side of the island, which offers good views.

Eating Out

Paris is often described as the capital of gastronomy, so a meal out in the city has a lot to live up to. The standard for the best restaurants–the Michelin rosette–is famed throughout the world as the epitome of gastronomic excellence.

Budget Choices

If your budget isn't up to the crème-de-la-crème, there are hundreds of less expensive choices, from regional French cuisine to North African, Lebanese or Japanese. Be prepared to take time over your meal–good food is to be enjoyed.

The Very Best

Restaurants have higher prices than brasseries or bistros but will often provide a refined setting, elegant cuisine and a good wine list. For a special treat, look for multi-starred Michelin chefs such as Alain Ducasse and Guy Savoy. Dress smartly and book in advance.

Lunch and Snacks

Cafés and bars serve coffee, tea, soft drinks, alcohol and snacks. Most open from around 9am until well into the evening and many have outdoor seating. *Salons de thé* (tea rooms) open from noon until evening. If you are on a budget, have your main meal at lunchtime, when most restaurants serve a reasonably priced *menu du jour*, or daily menu, of two or three courses with a glass of wine.

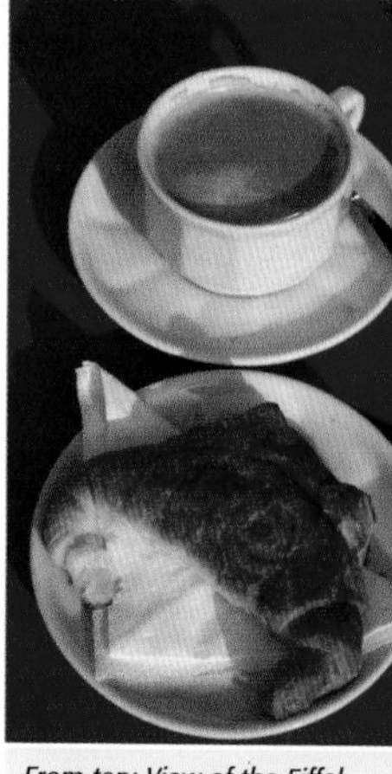

From top: View of the Eiffel Tower from Le Totem; champagne; table setting; coffee and a croissant

OPENING TIMES

Most restaurants and bistros keep strict serving times. Restaurants open at 12, close at 2.30, then reopen at 7.30 or 8. Most Parisians take an hour for lunch and eat in the staff canteen or in a local bistro. The evening meal is the most important of the day and is usually taken *en famille* between 8 and 9pm. Restaurants stop taking orders between 10 and 11pm. To eat later, try the Les Halles area or a brasserie. Some restaurants close on weekends and in July and August.

Restaurants by Cuisine

There are restaurants to suit all tastes and budgets in Paris. On this page they are listed by cuisine. For a more detailed description of each restaurant, see Paris by Area.

ASIAN

Benkay (▷ 36)
Yugaraj (▷ 56)

FRENCH-BISTRO

L'Affriolé (▷ 36)
Au Pied du Cochon (▷ 70)
Au Virage Lepic (▷ 96)
Bistrot L'Oulette (▷ 70)
Bistro Poulbot (▷ 96)
Café Burq (▷ 96)
Café des Musées (▷ 70)
Café Marly (▷ 86)
Chez Grisette (▷ 96)
Chez Jean (▷ 96)
Le Comptoir (▷ 56)
Le Cristal de Sel (▷ 36)
Croquembouche (▷ 106)
L'Entêtée (▷ 36)
Louis Vins (▷ 56)
La Muse Vin (▷ 70)
Le Petit Saint-Benoît (▷ 56)
Pramil (▷ 70)
Le Progès (▷ 96)
Le Soleil (▷ 106)

FRENCH-BRASSERIE

Bofinger (▷ 70)
Le Capitainerie (▷ 106)
Chalet des Îles (▷ 106)
La Coupole (▷ 56)
La Guinguette de Neuilly (▷ 106)
La Tête Ailleurs (▷ 70)
Thoumieux (▷ 36)

FRENCH-ELEGANT

Le Céladon (▷ 86)
Le Ciel de Paris (▷ 36)
Le Clarisse (▷ 36)
La Grande Cascade (▷ 106)
Guy Savoy (▷ 86)
Jacques Cagna (▷ 56)
Le Jules Verne (▷ 36)
Pré Catalan (▷ 106)
Taillevent (▷ 86)
La Tour d'Argent (▷ 56)

FRENCH-REGIONAL

L'Ami Jean (▷ 36)
Au Clair de la Lune (▷ 96)
Benoit (▷ 70)
Carré des Feuillants (▷ 86)

FUSION

6 New York (▷ 86)
Spoon (▷ 86)

ITALIAN

Bistro Romain (▷ 86)
Sole Caffe & Cucina (▷ 96)

NORTH AFRICAN

404 (▷ 70)

TRENDY

Alcazar (▷ 56)
Georges (▷ 70)
Kitchen Galerie Bis (▷ 56)
La Mère Lachaise (▷ 106)
Monjul (▷ 70)
Rose Bakery (▷ 96)
Le Senderens (▷ 86)
Ze Kitchen Galerie (▷ 56)

If You Like...

However you'd like to spend your time in Paris, these top suggestions should help you tailor your ideal visit. Each suggestion has a fuller write-up elsewhere in the book.

ANTIQUING

Hunt for a bargain at the Marché aux Puces de Saint-Ouen (▷ 100), an immense weekend flea market.

Travel to Asia without leaving Paris at Galerie Captier (▷ 35), where you'll find antique Chinese furniture and Japanese screens.

Pick up a poster or etching by Toulouse-Lautrec at Galerie Documents (▷ 54).

Visit the warren of antiques shops at the Louvre des Antiquaires (▷ 84).

Shop at markets and high-end stores or enjoy the superb cuisine in Paris's restaurants

HAUTE COUTURE

Check out the fashions by knitwear queen Sonia Rykiel (▷ 54).

Find a wide selection of designer clothing at the department stores Le Bon Marché Rive Gauche (▷ 35), Galeries Lafayette or Printemps (▷ 84, panel).

Try on original yet timeless styles at Colette (▷ 84): it's cutting-edge and very exclusive.

Top off your look with one of Marie Mercié's fabulous hats (▷ 54).

FINE DINING

Sample the super-refined cuisine and exquisite wines at the Pré Catelan (▷ 106), in the Bois de Boulogne.

Find out how Guy Savoy turns cooking into an art form at his eponymous restaurant (▷ 86).

Dine at Le Senderens, the Michelin-starred restaurant of Alain Senderens (▷ 86).

Try the latest trends in fusion foods as interpreted by Alain Ducasse at Spoon (▷ 86).

Enjoy the varied nightlife in Paris—bars, theatres, clubs, opera, ballet: It's all here

ALL-NIGHT ANTICS

Spot the celebs at trendy club Le Baron (▷ 85).

Drink martinis into the wee hours in the old-fashioned New World ambience of Harry's New York Bar (▷ 85).

Dance the night away at Folie's Pigalle (▷ 95).

Descend into the medieval basement at Caveau de la Huchette for a high-ambience concert (▷ 55).

Take in a concert at the Divan du Monde (▷ 95) and stay on afterwards to hear guest DJs.

CATERING TO THE KIDDIES

Ride the glass elevator to the top of the Eiffel Tower (▷ 30–31).

Rent a toy sailboat and launch it in the fountain in the Jardin du Luxembourg (▷ 42).

Explore interactive exhibitions at the Cité des Sciences et de l'Industrie in the Parc de la Villette (▷ 104).

Set the little darlings loose in the Si Tu Veux toy shop (▷ 84).

There is plenty for young people to enjoy in the city

SHOESTRING PLEASURES

There's free admission to the permanent collections of all city-run museums: the Musée Carnavalet (▷ 62), Musée d'Art Moderne de la Ville de Paris (▷ 33) and many more.

Picnic on a bench on the Pont des Arts pedestrian bridge and watch the boats pass below while the crowds pass in front of you (▷ 82).

Visit the Atelier Brancusi, a reconstruction of sculptor Constantin Brancusi's workshop, in front of the Centre Georges Pompidou (▷ 60), for free.

BIRD'S-EYE VIEWS

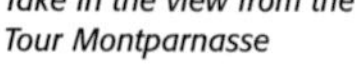

Take in the view from the Tour Montparnasse

Stop shopping long enough to check out the view from Printemps de la Maison's ninth floor (▷ 84, panel).

See what the city looks like from central Paris's only skyscraper, the Tour Montparnasse (▷ 34).

Admire the view from the dome of Sacré-Cœur (▷ 90–91).

Have a meal at the Eiffel Tower's Le Jules Verne restaurant (▷ 36).

LAZY MORNINGS

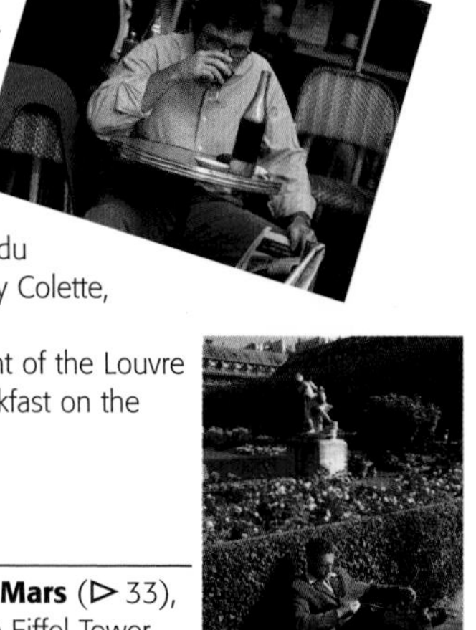

Cruise down the Seine in a *bateau mouche* (▷ 48–49).

Commune with the ghosts of Sartre and Hemingway at the Café de Flore (▷ 50).

Sit by the fountain in the Jardin du Palais Royal (▷ 81) with a book by Colette, who once lived there.

Watch the tourists line up in front of the Louvre pyramid while you linger over breakfast on the terrace of the Café Marly (▷ 86).

A quiet moment in the gardens of the Palais Royal

GOING FOR THE GREEN

Frolic in the Parc du Champ de Mars (▷ 33), a huge stretch of lawn beneath the Eiffel Tower.

Admire the statues as you wander through the stately Jardin du Luxembourg (▷ 42).

Look for the grave of one of your heroes—whether Jim Morrison or Marcel Proust—in the park-like Père Lachaise cemetery (▷ 102).

Find out what landscape designers do when they create a modern urban park on a former industrial estate at Parc André-Citroën (▷ 104).

Visit the Parc de la Villette, Paris's largest green space (▷ 104).

The Jardin des Tuileries is a popular place to enjoy the sunshine during the summer

Paris by Area

Around the Tour Eiffel

Home to the symbol of Paris and its most famous tourist attraction, the Eiffel Tower, along with several other important monuments and museums, this is primarily a staid, well-to-do residential district.

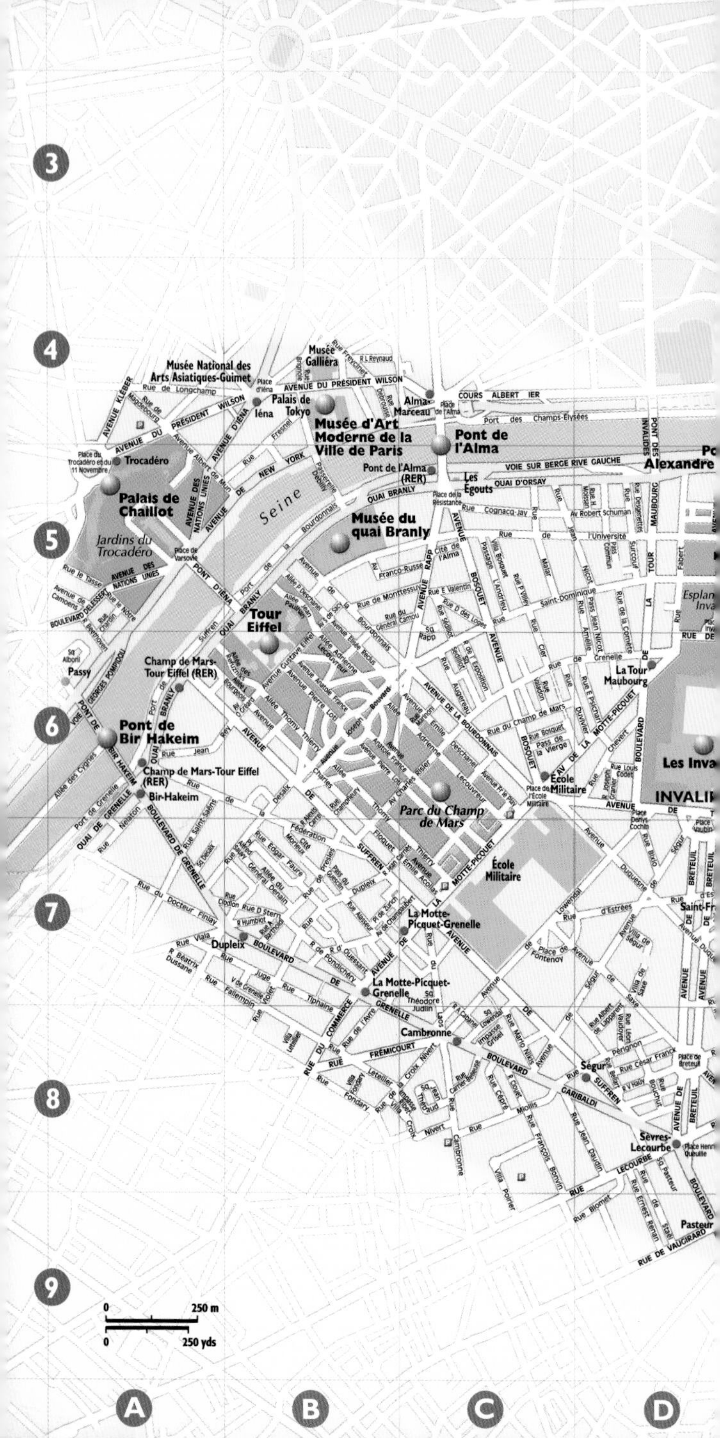

3
4
5
6
7
8
9
A
B
C
D
Musée National des Arts Asiatiques-Guimet
Musée Galliéra
Palais de Tokyo
Musée d'Art Moderne de la Ville de Paris
Pont de l'Alma
Alma-Marceau
Iéna
Trocadéro
Palais de Chaillot
Jardins du Trocadéro
Seine
Musée du quai Branly
Tour Eiffel
Champ de Mars-Tour Eiffel (RER)
Pont de Bir Hakeim
Champ de Mars-Tour Eiffel (RER)
Bir-Hakeim
Passy
Pont de l'Alma (RER)
Les Égouts
Pont Alexandre
Esplanade des Invalides
La Tour Maubourg
Les Invalides
École Militaire
Parc du Champ de Mars
École Militaire
La Motte-Picquet-Grenelle
La Motte-Picquet-Grenelle
Dupleix
Cambronne
Ségur
Sèvres-Lecourbe
Pasteur
Saint-François-Xavier
AVENUE DU PRÉSIDENT WILSON
COURS ALBERT IER
Port des Champs-Elysées
VOIE SUR BERGE RIVE GAUCHE
QUAI D'ORSAY
QUAI BRANLY
PONT D'IÉNA
AVENUE RAPP
AVENUE BOSQUET
AVENUE DE LA BOURDONNAIS
AVENUE DE LA MOTTE-PICQUET
AVENUE DE SUFFREN
BOULEVARD DE GRENELLE
QUAI DE GRENELLE
BOULEVARD GARIBALDI
RUE DU COMMERCE
RUE LECOURBE
RUE DE VAUGIRARD
Rue de l'Université
Rue Saint-Dominique
Rue Cler
Avenue de Ségur
Avenue Duquesne
Place de Fontenoy
Allée des Cygnes
0
250 m
0
250 yds

Around the Tour Eiffel

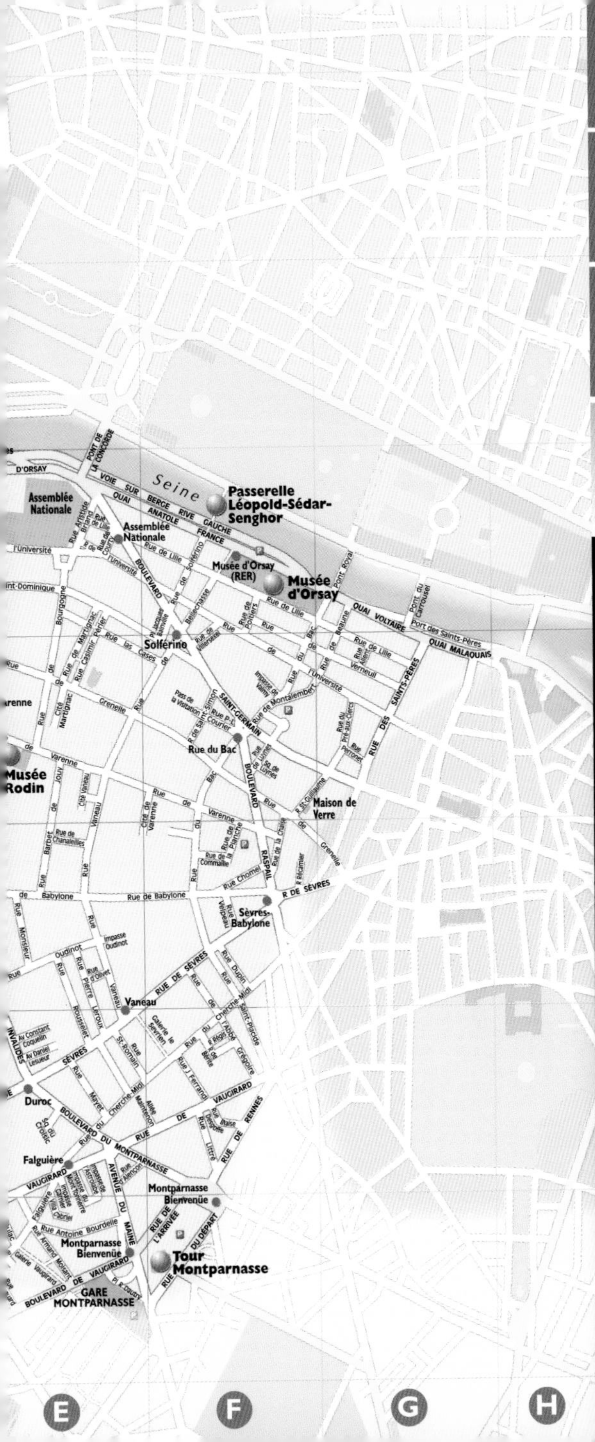

E F G H

Les Invalides

TOP 25

HIGHLIGHTS

- 195m-wide (640ft) facade
- Sword and armour of François I
- Napoleon's stuffed horse
- *Emperor Napoleon*, Ingres
- Napoleon's tomb
- Église du Dôme
- A Renault light tank
- Dragon mask in Oriental collection
- World War II exhibition

TIPS

- For the best views, arrive via the Pont Alexandre III.
- Your ticket also gives you a discount at the Musée Rodin.

The gilded dome rising above the Hôtel des Invalides recalls the pomp and glory of France's two greatest promoters—the Sun King, who built it, and the power-hungry Napoleon Bonaparte, who is entombed there.

Glory The vast, imposing edifice of Les Invalides was built to house invalid soldiers and it continues to accommodate a few today. Its classical facade and majestic Cour d'Honneur date from the 1670s, with the ornate Église du Dôme completed in 1706 and the long grassy esplanade established soon after. The home of military institutions, Les Invalides is also a memorial to the succession of battles and campaigns that have marked French history and which are illustrated in the Musée de l'Armée. Here is Napoleon's frock coat, hat,

Clockwise from top left: A view of the extensive facade of Les Invalides; a cannon in the courtyard; an unusual image of the dome against a statue; night-time view of Les Invalides with its gilded dome

coronation saddle and even his actual horse, Vizir (not for the squeamish). There is also a re-creation of the room where he died in exile on the island of St-Helena. You can also see the armour of François I and the intriguing Oriental collection, complete with a dragon mask for horses. Don't miss the poignant World War II exhibition, which moves chronologically through the war years over three floors in the west wing. The evocative displays use film footage, photos and day-to-day objects.

Tombs The baroque cupolas, arches, columns and sculptures of the Église du Dôme highlight France's military achievements and heroes. Tombs of generals fill the chapels, while the crypt contains Napoleon's grandiose sarcophagus, guarded by 12 statues, symbols of his military campaigns.

THE BASICS

www.invalides.org
D6
129 rue de Grenelle, 75007
Musée de l'Armée 01 44 42 38 77
Apr–end Sep daily 10–6; Oct–end Mar 10–5. Closed first Mon of month (except Jul–Sep). Église du Dôme open until 7 Jul, Aug
La Tour Maubourg, Invalides, Varenne
28, 49, 63, 69, 83, 87, 92, 93
RER Line C, Invalides
Partial access
Moderate
For guided tours for groups call 01 44 42 37 72

Musée d'Orsay

HIGHLIGHTS

- *Olympia*, Manet
- *Déjeuner sur l'Herbe*, Edouard Manet
- *Orphée*, Gustave Moreau
- *La Mère*, James McNeill Whistler
- *L'Angélus*, Jean-François Millet
- *La Cathédrale de Rouen*, Claude Monet
- *Dans un Café*, Edgar Degas
- *La Chambre à Arles*, Vincent Van Gogh
- *Femmes de Tahiti*, Paul Gauguin
- Chair by Charles Rennie Mackintosh

TIP

- A Paris Museum Pass (▷ 122) allows you to skip the queues for tickets.

You'll either love or hate the conversion of this 1900 train station. But whatever your view, its art collections, covering the years from 1848 to 1914, are a must for anyone interested in this crucial art period.

Monolithic When this museum finally opened in 1986 controversy ran high: Gae Aulenti's heavy stone structures lay unhappily under Laloux's delicate iron-and-glass shell, built as a train terminus in 1900. But the collections redeem this faux pas, offering a solid overview of the momentous period from Romanticism to Fauvism. After exploring the 19th-century paintings, sculptures and decorative arts at ground level, it's time for the Impressionist and post-Impressionist schools (due to be displayed on the upper and middle levels after the museum's

Clockwise from far left: The dimensions of the former railway station are evident here; an airy space for Impressionist paintings; looking out through the clock face; viewing sculptures; The Midday Siesta *by Vincent Van Gogh; copying the work of a master*

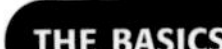

renovation is completed). Works by the giants of French art—Degas, Monet, Cézanne, Van Gogh, Renoir, Sisley and Pissarro—are the biggest crowd pullers. Don't miss the views from the outside terrace and café behind the station clock at the top.

Other highlights You can also see paintings that are examples of Naturalism, Symbolism and the Nabis school. There are sculptures by Rodin, Émile-Antoine Bourdelle and Aristide Maillol, and art nouveau furniture. Save time for the Salle des Fêtes (room 51), tucked away at the end of the middle level. The extravagantly chandeliered and mirrored room was originally part of the station's hotel.

All change Renovation work has led to the closure of the Impressionist rooms until some time in 2011. The exhibits are on show elsewhere in the museum.

THE BASICS

www.musee-orsay.fr

F5

1 rue de la Légion d'Honneur, 75007

01 40 49 48 00 or 01 40 49 48 14

Tue–Sun 9.30–6, Thu 9.30–9.45

Café des Hauteurs on upper level; plush restaurant/tea room on middle level; snack bar

Solférino

24, 63, 68, 69, 73, 83, 84, 94

RER Line C, Musée d'Orsay

Excellent

Moderate; free first Sun of each month

Audio and guided tours, concerts and lectures

Musée du quai Branly

Greenery and glass walls decorate the exterior of the museum

THE BASICS

www.quaibranly.fr
B5
29–37 quai Branly, 75007
01 56 61 70 00
Sun, Tue, Wed 11–7, Thu–Sat 11–9
Gourmet restaurant Les Ombres on the roof terrace (01 47 53 68 00) and Café Branly in the garden
Pont de l'Alma, Alma-Marceau
42, 63, 72, 80, 92
Good
Moderate (gardens free)

HIGHLIGHTS

- A glass tower of 9,000 musical instruments
- Gabonese masks
- Aztec statues
- Rare Ethiopian frescoes
- Feather headdresses and painted animal hides from the Americas
- The Harter bequest of masks and sculptures from the Cameroon

This museum, which opened in 2006 near the Seine and Eiffel Tower, is dedicated to the cultural heritage of Africa, Asia, Oceania and the Americas.

A 21st-century venue Built on five levels and crowned by a wide terrace with fine views of the Eiffel Tower, the museum is hidden from view by trees and thick vegetation. *Le mur végétal* (plant wall) festoons the north facade, with 15,000 plants representing 150 species from all over the world.

Inside A swooping white ramp leads through a dark tunnel before reaching the display area, where you are greeted by a 10th-century anthropomorphic Dogon wood statue from Mali, its one remaining arm reaching skywards. This splendid beginning sets the tone for other highlights, including painted animal hides from the Americas, decorated with battle scenes and abstract earth and sky motifs; a glass tower of 9,000 musical instruments that have been gathered from all corners of the world; and a headdress from Malekula Island, worn by dancers during rituals in the early 20th century. To aid navigation through the museum, each of the different regions has its own floor colouring.

Other attractions Ten temporary exhibitions are staged each year. There's also live entertainment in the theatre. The quai Branly's Open University, which is accessible to everyone, organizes debates on historic and contemporary issues and encourages dialogue through its series of lectures.

The Thinker *by Rodin (left); more works by Rodin inside the museum (right)*

Musée Rodin

As an antidote to the military might of Les Invalides (▷ 24–25), wander into the enchanting Musée Rodin, which is often forgotten by Parisians.

Hard times This rococo mansion, built for a wig-maker in 1730, has an interesting history. One owner (the Duc de Lauzun) was sent to the guillotine and the house has been used successively as a dance hall, convent, school and artists' studios. Rodin lived here from 1908 until his death in 1917. In 1919 the house became a museum. The renovated chapel on the grounds is now used for temporary exhibitions.

Sculpture The elegant, luminous interior houses the collection that Rodin left to the nation. It ranges from his early sketches to the later watercolours and includes many of his most celebrated white marble and bronze sculptures, including *The Kiss* (*Le Baiser*). There are busts of the composer Mahler and writer Victor Hugo, among others, and a series of studies of Balzac. Alongside the Rodins are works by his contemporaries, in particular his tragic mistress and model, Camille Claudel, as well as Eugène Carrière, Edvard Munch, Renoir, Monet and Van Gogh. Rodin's furniture and antiques complete this exceptional collection.

Retreat The museum's private gardens are Paris's third largest and contain several major sculptures, a pond, flowering shrubs and benches for a quiet read. It's worth buying the garden-only ticket just for a respite from city life.

THE BASICS

www.musee-rodin.fr
E6
79 rue de Varenne, 75007
01 44 18 61 10
Apr–end Sep Tue–Sun 9.30–5.45; Oct–end Mar Tue–Sun 9.30–4.45 (gardens open until 6.45 in summer; last entry at 5.15)
Peaceful garden café
Varenne, Invalides
69, 82, 87, 92
Wheelchair access
Moderate (garden inexpensive)

HIGHLIGHTS

- *Les Bourgeois de Calais (The Burghers of Calais)*
- *Le Penseur (The Thinker)*
- *La Porte de l'Enfer (The Gates of Hell)*
- *Le Baiser (The Kiss)*
- *La Main de Dieu (The Hand of God)*
- *Adam et Eve*
- *Ugolin*
- *Le Père Tanguy*, Van Gogh
- Original staircase

Tour Eiffel

TOP 25

HIGHLIGHTS

- Panoramic views
- Bust of Gustave Eiffel
- Sparkling lights

TIPS

- To skip the wait for the elevators, walk up the stairs to level two, then catch the elevator to the top. The climb isn't too daunting.
- The wait for the elevator is generally shorter at night.
- Pushchairs (strollers) are allowed up the tower only if they are collapsible.

The Eiffel Tower could be a cliché but it isn't. The powerful silhouette of Gustave Eiffel's marvel of engineering still makes a stirring sight, especially at night when its delicate, lace-like iron structure comes to the fore.

Glittering feat Built in a record two years for the 1889 Exposition Universelle, the controversial Eiffel Tower was never intended to be a permanent feature of the city. However, in 1910 it was finally saved for posterity, preparing the way for today's 6.7 million annual visitors. Avoid a long wait for the elevator by visiting the tower at night, when it fully lives up to its romantic image and provides a glittering spectacle—whether the illumination from the tower itself or the carpet of nocturnal Paris unfolding at its feet. More than

Clockwise from top left: Underneath the Eiffel Tower; the tower at night, with the fountains of the Palais de Chaillot in the foreground; another view from below; the panoramic view from the tower; illuminated at night

330 spotlights illuminate the latticework, topped by a rotating beacon that can be seen up to 80km (50 miles) away. After dusk the tower sparkles for 10 minutes every hour on the hour until 2am.

Violent reactions Gustave Eiffel was a master of cast-iron structures, his prolific output included hundreds of factories, churches, viaducts and bridges on four continents. His 324m (1,063ft) tower attracted great opposition, but his genius was vindicated by the fact that it sways no more than 9cm (3.5in) in high winds and remained the world's highest structure for 40 years. Eiffel kept an office here until his death in 1923; he may have seen Comte de Lambert circle above in a flying-machine in 1909, or a modern-day Icarus testing a wearable parachute plummet to his death from the parapet in 1912.

THE BASICS

www.tour-eiffel.fr
B6
Quai Branly, Champ de Mars, 75007
01 44 11 23 23
Sep to mid-Jun 9.30am–11pm (stairs 9.30–6.30); mid-Jun to end Aug daily 9am–midnight; last admission 30 mins before closing
Altitude 95 (1st floor, 01 45 55 20 04); Jules Verne (2nd floor, ▷ 36)
Bir-Hakeim, Trocadéro
42, 69, 72, 82, 87
RER Line C, Tour Eiffel
Very good (to 2nd floor)
Expensive; stairs moderate

Palais de Chaillot

Gold statues outside the Palais (left); an exhibit in the Musée de la Marine (right)

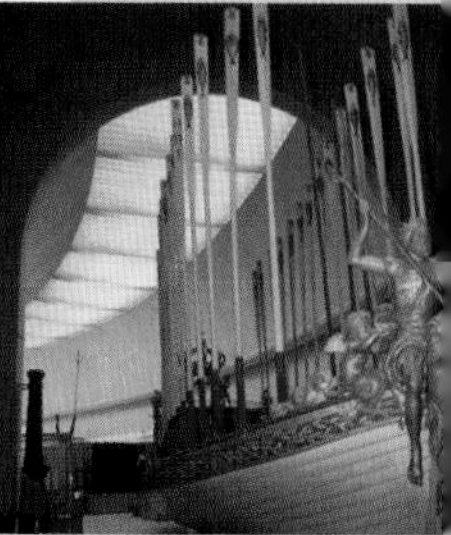

THE BASICS

A5
Place du Trocadéro, 75116
Marine 01 53 65 69 69; www.musee-marine.fr
Homme 01 44 05 72 72; www.mnhn.fr
Cité 01 58 51 52 00; www.citechaillot.fr
Marine Wed–Mon 10–6; Homme closed for renovation; Cité Wed–Mon 11–7 (until 9 Thu)
Café Carlu, in the Pavilion de Tête
Trocadéro
22, 30, 32, 63, 72, 82
Good
Moderate

HIGHLIGHTS

Marine

- View of the Eiffel Tower
- Napoleon's imperial barge
- *Ports de France*, Vernet
- *Le Valmy*

Cité

- *Vierges Folles*, on the tympanum of the Cathedral of Strasbourg

With its majestic wings curving towards the Eiffel Tower, and its monumental presence, the Palais de Chaillot attracts mime artists, skaters and promenaders.

Attractions The 1937 Exposition Universelle instigated the Palais de Chaillot's columns, which are punctuated with bronze statues that overlook terraces and fountains. This spectacular art deco wrapping contains three museums and the Théatre de Chaillot. The west wing houses the Musée de la Marine, one of the largest maritime and naval museums in the world, and the Musée de l'Homme, devoted to anthropology and ethnogrophy but closed for renovation until 2012. A large part of its ethnological collection has now been transferred to the new Musée du quai Branly (▷ 28).

Architecture and monuments The year 2007 saw the reopening of the revamped east wing of the building, which now houses the Cité de l'Architecture et du Patrimoine. On the ground floor the Galerie des Moulages displays more than 350 life-size plaster casts and 60 maquettes of architecture, including entire portals of churches and cathedrals such as Chartres. On the second level the Galerie d'Architecture Moderne et Contemporaine charts developments from the 1850s to the present day.

Looking out Through the tall windows, there are stunning views of the Trocadéro fountains, the Eiffel Tower and the Seine.

More to See

MUSÉE D'ART MODERNE DE LA VILLE DE PARIS

www.mam.paris.fr

Outstanding temporary exhibitions help keep this modern-art museum within an international sphere. The collection covers Fauvism, Cubism, Surrealism, Abstraction and Nouveau Réalisme. *La Danse* (1932), a mural by Henri Matisse, hangs in a room devoted to the artist. Next door to the museum, the Palais de Tokyo (▷ 35) houses the Centre d'Art Contemporain.

B4 11 avenue du Président Wilson, 75016 01 53 67 40 00 Tue, Wed 10–6, Thu 10–10, Fri–Sun 10–6 Iéna, Alma-Marceau Free. Temporary exhibitions: moderate

PARC DU CHAMP DE MARS

The lawns of the Champ de Mars stretch out in a rectangular design between the Eiffel Tower and the 18th-century École Militaire. The Romans fought the Celtic Parisii tribe here in 52BC—the park's name, Field of Mars, refers to the Roman god of war. It wasn't until 1765 that the site became a parade ground for the École Militaire's young cadets. The park has hosted national celebrations, parades, international exhibitions, horse races and early hot-air ballooning experiments. Today it is popular with families, joggers and visitors.

C6 Champ de Mars, 75007 École Militaire

PASSERELLE LÉOPOLD-SÉDAR-SENGHOR

This handsome modern wooden footbridge connects the Musée d'Orsay with the Tuileries garden. Its benches provide a pleasant place to sit and enjoy the river views.

F5 Quai des Tuileries/quai Anatole France Solferino

PONT ALEXANDRE III

Four gilded bronze Pegasus figures watch over this wildly ornate bridge, which forms a link between Les Invalides (▷ 24–25) on the Left Bank and the Grand Palais and Petit Palais on the Right. Symbolic of the optimism of the Belle Époque, it was built

Relaxing in the Champ de Mars

The Palais de Tokyo is home to the Centre d'Art Contemporain

for the 1900 Exposition Universelle. The bridge is crammed with elaborate decoration by more than 15 artists.
D4 Cours de la Reine/quai d'Orsay Invalides, Champs-Élysées–Clémenceau

PONT DE L'ALMA

The first Pont de l'Alma was built in 1856 to commemorate a victory over the Russians by the Franco-British alliance in the Crimean War. The bridge was replaced in 1974. The underpass on the Right Bank is where the fatal car crash involving Diana, Princess of Wales, occurred in August 1997. The Liberty Flame near the entrance, a symbol of American and French friendship, has become an unofficial memorial.
C4/C5 Place de l'Alma/place de la Résistance Alma-Marceau

PONT DE BIR-HAKEIM

The bridge was built between 1903 and 1905. The two-tier art nouveau structure has a walkway, roadway and a Métro viaduct. It is made up of two unequal metal structures on either side of the allée des Cygnes. The bridge was given its name in 1949, in memory of the victory of General Koenig in Libya in 1942.
A6 Quai Branly/avenue du Président Kennedy Bir-Hakeim, Passy

TOUR MONTPARNASSE

www.tourmontparnasse56.com
When it was constructed in 1973, the Tour Montparnasse's 59 floors of smoked glass and steel provoked cries of indignation. Since then it has become a familiar landmark, visible from all over Paris and spectacular by night, when hundreds of windows light up the sky. The 56th-floor viewing gallery and the 59th-floor terrace of this 209m (685ft) tower offer breathtaking views of the city. On a clear day you can see up to 40km (25 miles) away. Films on Paris (in French) are screened on the 56th floor.
F9 33 avenue du Maine, 75015 01 45 38 52 56 Apr–end Sep daily 9.30am–11.30pm; Oct–end Mar 9.30am–10.30pm (until 11 Fri, Sat). Last elevator up is 30 mins before closing Montparnasse-Bienvenüe Moderate

Tour Montparnasse (above)
Pont de Bir-Hakeim (above right)

Statues on Pont Alexandre III

Shopping

LE BON MARCHÉ RIVE GAUCHE

www.lebonmarche.fr
You'll find the classiest goods in this Left-Bank store. The modernist interior adds to the elegant atmosphere. Don't miss the beauty shop, appropriately named 'Théâtre de la Beauté', on the ground floor and the food hall, La Grande Epicerie, in an adjoining building, stocking delicacies from all over the world.
F7 24 rue de Sèvres, 75007 01 44 39 80 00 Mon–Wed 10–7.30, Thu 10–9, Fri 10–8, Sat 9.30–8 Sèvres-Babylone, Vaneau

THE CONRAN SHOP

English designer Sir Terence Conran is a hit with the Parisian crowd. Fine materials, a post-1970s influence and sometimes an ethnic twist give Conran's furniture a modern elegance. Bathroom, kitchen and garden accessories complete the range. A small selection of fine foods from all over the world is also sold in this superb building, designed by Gustave Eiffel.
F7 117 rue du Bac, 75007 01 42 84 10 01 Mon–Fri 10–7, Sat 10–7.30 Sèvres-Babylone

GALERIE CAPTIER

The antique Chinese furniture (17th to 19th century) and old Japanese screens here have been chosen by owners Bernard and Sylvie Captier, who regularly travel to Asia to search out exotic and refined works of art.
G6 33 rue de Beaune, 75007 01 42 61 00 57 Mon 2.30–7, Tue–Sat 10.30–7 Rue du Bac

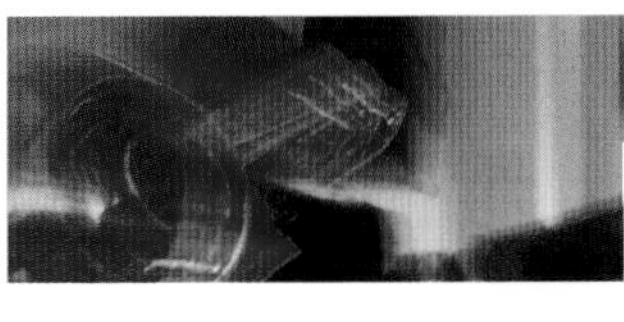

Entertainment and Nightlife

LA PAGODE

A film theatre inside an oriental pagoda shows cult classics and modern films in their original language. There's an adjoining garden.
E7 57 bis rue de Babylone, 75007 01 45 55 48 48 Varies Saint-François Xavier

PALAIS DE TOKYO

www.palaisdetokyo.com
Dedicated to the most avant-garde contemporary art, this venue is attempting to revive the spirit of Andy Warhol's factory. The large space, with its exposed concrete interior, hosts temporary exhibitions, concerts, film projections and debates.
B4 13 avenue du Président Wilson, 75016 01 47 23 54 01 Tue–Sun 12–12 Iéna, Alma-Marceau, Trocadéro

CINEPHILE'S PARADISE

Paris must be the cinema-going capital of the world. With some 350 films shown each day, the choice can be tantalizing. Foreign films shown in their original languages have 'VO' (*version originale*) after the title. New films come out on Wednesday, but you'll also find an amazing selection of older and classic films in art houses. The Gaumont, MK2 and UGC cinemas offer multiple-entry cards that can be used for up to three people and can save you precious euros.

PETIT JOURNAL MONTPARNASSE

This club, sister venue to the Petit Journal Saint-Michel, has hosted some of France's best-loved jazz musicians, and you can dine while listening or just have a drink.
E9 13 rue Commandant-Mouchotte, 75014 01 43 21 56 70 Closed Sun Montparnasse-Bienvenüe

Restaurants

PRICES

Prices are approximate, based on a 3-course meal for one person.

€€€	over €90
€€	€30–€90
€	under €30

L'AFFRIOLÉ (€–€€)

This popular 'nouveau bistro' offers great value for the money, friendly service and classic French dishes with a twist (such as pig's-feet croquettes or pork ribs in red wine).
C5 17 rue Malar, 75007 01 44 18 31 33 Tue–Sat lunch, dinner Pont de l'Alma, Invalides

L'AMI JEAN (€€)

Unassuming, friendly restaurant specializing in Basque dishes. Veal, beef and seafood are enhanced by fine wines.
C5 27 rue Malar, 75007 01 47 05 86 89 Tue–Sat lunch, dinner Pont de l'Alma, La Tour Maubourg

BENKAY (€€)

A modern Japanese restaurant with panoramic views from the 4th floor of the Novotel Paris Tour Eiffel. Good teppan-yaki.
A7 61 quai de Grenelle, 75015 01 40 58 21 26 Daily lunch, dinner Bir-Hakeim

LE CIEL DE PARIS (€€)

On the 56th floor of the Tour Montparnasse, this is the highest restaurant in Paris. The menu changes with the seasons, but may include pan-sautéed fillet of beef with a truffle sauce, lobster risotto, or fried scallops with a parsley purée.
F9 Tour Montparnasse, 33 avenue du Maine, 75015 01 40 64 77 64 Daily lunch, dinner Montparnasse-Bienvenüe

LE CLARISSE (€€)

www.leclarisse.fr

Understated black-and-white design sets the scene for hearty yet refined dishes from chef Arnaud Mene—creamy wild mushroom soup and slow-cooked hare in winter—followed by classic French desserts.
D5 29 rue Surcouf, 75007 01 45 50 11 10 Mon–Fri lunch, dinner, Sat dinner only Invalides

LE CRISTAL DE SEL (€€)

Watch chef Karil Lopez in his tiny kitchen as he turns out simple, fresh, satisfying food in this popular restaurant.
Off map 13 rue Mademoiselle, 75015 01 42 50 35 29 Tue–Sat lunch, dinner Commerce

FRENCH MEAN CUISINE

'The only cooks in the civilized world are French. Other races have different interpretations of food. Only the French understand cuisine because their qualities—rapidity, decision-making, tact—are used. Who has ever seen a foreigner succeed in making a white sauce?'—Nestor Roqueplan (1804–70), Editor of *Le Figaro*.

L'ENTÊTÉE (€)

The youthful Julie Ferrault turns out excellent French dishes with just the right hint of Asian taste in this tiny restaurant with simple, modern decor.
Off map 4 rue Danville, 75014 01 40 47 56 81 Tue–Fri lunch, dinner, Sat dinner Denfert Rochereau

LE JULES VERNE (€€€)

Alain Ducasse's Michelin-starred restaurant on level two of the Eiffel Tower is the talk of Paris. It has spectacular views and is popular and very expensive. Reservations are essential.
B6 2nd level, Tour Eiffel, 75007 (private elevator) 01 45 55 61 44 Daily lunch, dinner Bir-Hakeim

THOUMIEUX (€€)

Named after family proprietors, this brasserie, established in 1923, is near the Eiffel Tower. The elegant dining room has velvet wall seats and lots of mirrors. Expect hearty meals such as cassoulet (sausage and bean casserole) or duck dishes, including foie gras.
D5 79 rue Saint-Dominique, 75007 01 47 05 49 75 Mon–Sat 12–3, 7–11, Sun 12–11 Invalides

Latin Quarter, St-Germain & Islands

Ancient Paris grew out from the islands in the Seine. The Île de la Cité is the site of Notre-Dame, and residential Île Saint-Louis is one of the most picturesque spots in the city.

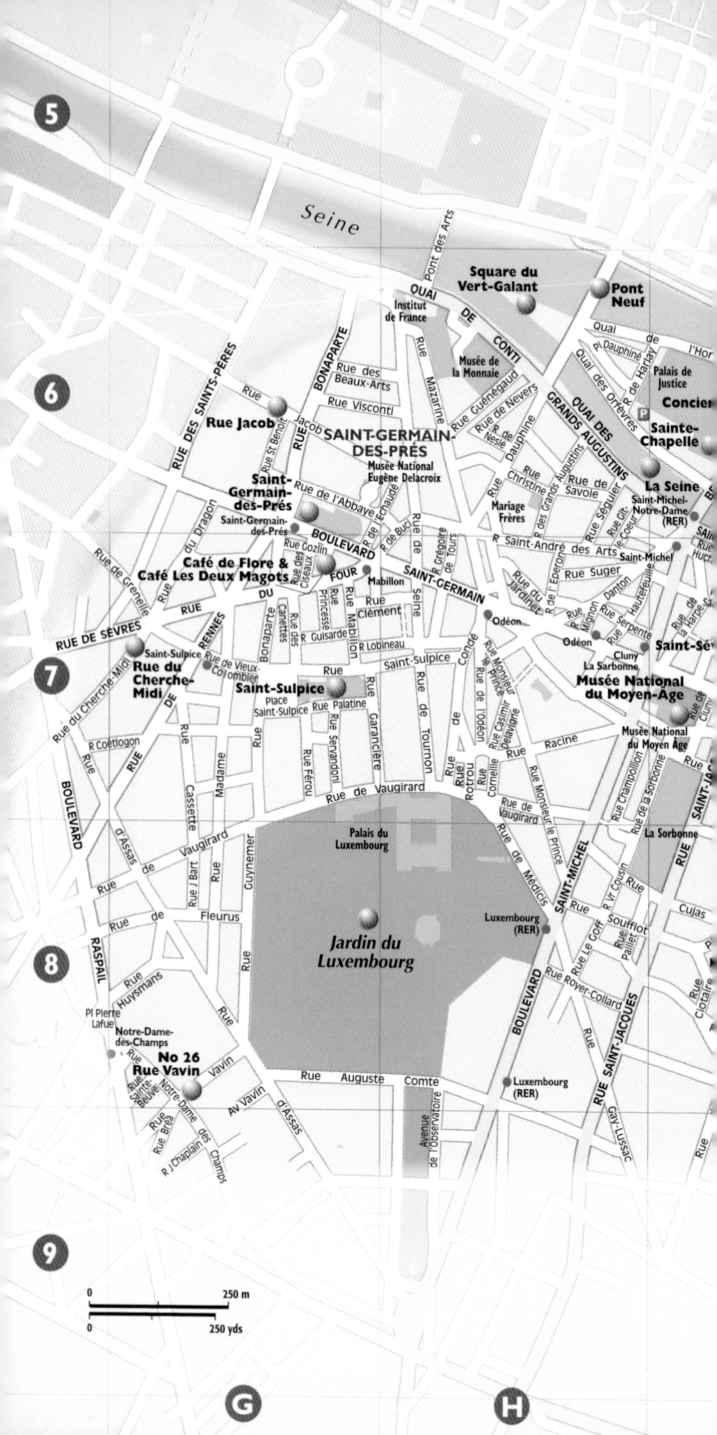

5
6
7
8
9
G
H
Seine
Square du Vert-Galant
Pont Neuf
Institut de France
Musée de la Monnaie
Palais de Justice
Sainte-Chapelle
Rue Jacob
SAINT-GERMAIN-DES-PRÉS
Musée National Eugène Delacroix
Saint-Germain-des-Prés
Café de Flore & Café Les Deux Magots
Mariage Frères
La Seine
Saint-Michel-Notre-Dame (RER)
Saint-Michel
Mabillon
Odéon
Cluny La Sorbonne
Musée National du Moyen-Âge
Musée National du Moyen Âge
Rue du Cherche-Midi
Saint-Sulpice
Place Saint-Sulpice
Palais du Luxembourg
Jardin du Luxembourg
Luxembourg (RER)
La Sorbonne
Notre-Dame-des-Champs
Pl Pierre Lafue
No 26 Rue Vavin
Avenue de l'Observatoire
Boulevard Saint-Germain
Boulevard Saint-Michel
Boulevard Raspail
Rue de Rennes
Rue de Vaugirard
Rue Saint-Jacques
0 250 m
0 250 yds

Pont Notre-Dame
Marché aux Fleurs
Île de la Cité
Rue de la Cité
Saint-Michel-Notre-Dame (RER)
Quai aux Fleurs
Rue d'Arcole
Rue des Ursins
Rue Chanoinesse
Pont Louis Philippe
Quai de Bourbon
Pont Marie
Pont Saint-Louis
Notre-Dame
Quai de Montebello
Rue Saint-Louis en l'Île
Quai d'Orléans
Île Saint-Louis
Quai d'Anjou
Pont de l'Archevêché
Mémorial des Martyrs de la Déportation
Quai de Béthune
Rue Poulletier
R des Deux Ponts
R Budé
Pont de la Tournelle
Quai de la Tournelle
Pont Sully
Bd Henri IV
Seine
Maubert-Mutualité
Boulevard Saint-Germain
Rue des Carmes
Rue de Bièvre
Rue des Bernardins
Rue de Pontoise
Rue Cochin
Rue de Poissy
Rue des Chantiers
Rue des Fossés Saint-Bernard
Institut du Monde Arabe
Quai Saint Bernard
Port Saint Bernard
Rue des Écoles
Sq P Langevin
Rue Saint-Victor
Rue Lemoine
QUARTIER LATIN
Rue Monge
Rue d'Arras
Rue du Cardinal Lemoine
Bibliothèque Nationale de France-François Mitterrand
Rue Laplace
St-Étienne-du-Mont
Pass Clopin
Rue Clovis
Rue Descartes
Cardinal Lemoine
Place Jussieu
Jussieu
Rue des Boulangers
Rue Jussieu
Rue Cuvier
Arènes de Lutèce
Rue des Arènes
Rue Linné
Rue Thouin
Rue Rollin
R Blainville
Place Monge
Rue de Navarre
Jardin des Plantes
Rue Lacepède
Rue St-Médard
Rue Mouffetard
R Ortolan
Rue Malus
Rue Gracieuse
Rue de la Clef
Rue de Quatrefages
Rue Geoffroy St-Hilaire
Muséum National d'Histoire Naturelle
Rue Tournefort
Rue Amyot
La Mosquée
R G Desplas
Rue Larrey
Hammam
Rue Daubenton
Rue Buffon
J
K
L

Conciergerie

HIGHLIGHTS

- Public clock
- Marie-Antoinette's cell
- Tour Bonbec
- Prisoners' cells upstairs

TIP

- If you also plan to visit Sainte-Chapelle (▷ 46–47), go to the Conciergerie first and buy a joint ticket, to avoid the queues at Sainte-Chapelle. But try to get to Sainte-Chapelle in the morning, before it gets very busy.

The ghosts of the victims of the guillotine must surely haunt this stark and gloomy place that served as a prison and torture chamber for more than five centuries and remains full of macabre mementoes of its grisly past.

From palace to prison Rising over the Seine in menacing grandeur, the turreted Conciergerie was built from 1299 to 1313 as part of a royal complex that also included Sainte-Chapelle. From 1391 until 1914 the building functioned as a prison and torture chamber, its reputation striking fear in the population. During the Revolution more than 4,000 prisoners were held here.

Relive history The boulevard du Palais entrance takes you into the hauntingly lit Salle des Gens

The Conciergerie at night (left) from the opposite side of the river and the Salle des Gens d'Armes (right), with its moody lighting

d'Armes. This is thought to be one of Europe's oldest surviving medieval halls and is where members of the royal household dined. From here a curious spiral staircase leads to the original kitchens. Off the Salle des Gens d'Armes is the gloomy Salle des Gardes; this sat below the Grand' Chambre, where the Revolutionary court dealt out countless death sentences. Across the corridor known as the rue de Paris is the Galerie des Prisonniers, where lawyers, prisoners and visitors mingled. Here is a re-creation of the concierge's and clerk's offices, as well as the Salle de Toilette, where prisoners were prepared for execution. At the far end is a poignant re-creation of Marie-Antoinette's cell. The eerie upstairs corridor has examples of the three types of cells available to prisoners, depending on their wealth. Another room lists the guillotine's 2,278 victims.

THE BASICS

www.conciergerie.monuments-nationaux.fr

J6

2 boulevard du Palais, Île de la Cité, 75001

01 53 40 60 97

Nov–end Feb daily 9–5; Mar–end Oct daily 9.30–6

Cité, Châtelet

21, 24, 38, 58, 81, 85

Moderate (joint ticket with Sainte-Chapelle expensive)

Guided tours daily

Jardin du Luxembourg

The gardens are always busy (left); a band playing at the bandstand (right)

THE BASICS

G8/H8

Main entrance place Edmond Restand, 75006 (various entrances)

Senate 01 42 34 20 00; www.senat.fr

Park 01 42 34 23 89

Daylight hours (times vary)

Open-air café, kiosk restaurant

Odéon

RER Line B, Luxembourg

21, 27, 38, 58, 82, 84, 85, 89, 96

Very good

Free

HIGHLIGHTS

- Médicis fountain
- *Cyclops*, *Acis* and *Galateus* sculptures
- Bandstand
- Statue of Delacroix
- Orange-tree conservatory
- Experimental fruit garden
- Beekeeping school
- Statues of queens of France

Despite the crowds, these gardens are serene in all weathers and are the epitome of French landscaping. The people who use them present an idealized image of an unhurried Parisian existence far from the daily truth of noise and traffic.

Layout Radiating from the large octagonal pond in front of the Palais du Luxembourg (now the Senate) are terraces, paths and a wide tree-lined alley that leads down to the Observatory crossroads. Natural attractions include shady chestnuts, potted orange and palm trees, lawns and even an experimental fruit garden and orchard, while fountains, tennis courts, beehives, a puppet theatre and children's playgrounds offer other distractions. Statues of the queens of France and artists and writers are dotted about. A plaque marks the oak tree planted in memory of the victims of 9/11.

Park activities All year round joggers pound the circumference and in summer sunbathers and bookworms settle into park chairs, card- and chess-players claim the shade in front of the Orangerie, bands tune up at the bandstand near the boulevard Saint-Michel entrance and children burn off energy on swings and donkey rides.

Inspiration The Palais du Luxembourg and gardens were commissioned by Marie de Médicis, wife of Henri IV, in 1615, and designed to resemble her childhood Florentine home. The Allée de l'Observatoire and the English-style garden were added in the early 19th century.

Decorative features on the exterior (left); the museum through a gateway (right)

Musée National du Moyen-Âge

Take a deep breath outside this museum, surrounded by re-created medieval gardens, and prepare to enter a time warp in which the days of troubadours and courtly love are conjured up.

Treasures The Gothic turreted Hôtel de Cluny was built at the end of the 15th century by Abbot Jacques d'Amboise and is one of France's finest examples of domestic architecture of this period. The museum it houses, also known as the Musée de Cluny, has 23,000 objects in its collection, most amassed by Alexandre du Sommerard, a 19th-century medievalist. The most famous piece is the beautiful *La Dame à la Licorne* tapestry (late 15th century). Costumes, accessories, textiles and tapestries are of Byzantine, Coptic or European origin, while the gold and metalwork room has outstanding pieces of Gallic, Barbarian, Merovingian and Visigothic artistry. Stained glass, table games, ceramics, wood carvings, illuminated manuscripts and Books of Hours, altarpieces and religious statuary complete this exceptional display.

Baths The late-Roman baths adjoining the Hôtel de Cluny, dating from the first to third centuries, are composed of three stone chambers: the Caldarium (steam bath), the Tepidarium (tepid bath) and the Frigidarium (cold bath), with ruins of the former gymnasium visible on the boulevard Saint-Germain side. Roman stonework is exhibited in the niches, while Room VIII houses 21 stone heads knocked from statues on the west front of Notre-Dame. A labyrinth of vaults can be toured.

THE BASICS

www.musee-moyenage.fr
J7
6 place Paul-Painlevé, 75005
01 53 73 78 00
Wed–Mon 9.15–5.45
Cluny-La Sorbonne
21, 27, 38, 63, 85, 86, 87, 96
Moderate
Guided tours of vaults, baths and collections in English: call ahead

HIGHLIGHTS

- *La Dame à la Licorne (The Lady and the Unicorn)* tapestries
- Gold altar frontal
- *Pilier des Nautes*
- Stone heads from Notre-Dame
- Medieval gardens
- Seventh-century votive crown
- Byzantine processional cross
- Stained glass
- Averbode altarpiece
- Abbot's Chapel

Notre-Dame

TOP 25

HIGHLIGHTS

- Views from the towers
- South rose window
- Porte Rouge
- Portail du Cloître
- The gargoyles
- Emmanuel bell
- Largest organ in Europe
- *Pietà*, Coustou
- Statue of Notre-Dame de Paris (14th-century Virgin and Child)

TIP

- Try to visit just before a service to experience the sense of anticipation as lights are turned on and people gather to worship.

Spectacular is the word to describe Paris's most extraordinary monument, with its 93m (305ft) spire and world-renowned flying buttresses. One of the finest views of the cathedral is from the *quais* to the east.

Evolution Construction started on this work of faith in 1163 and didn't finish until 1345, so the building ranges in style from Romanesque to Gothic. Since then the cathedral has suffered from pollution, politics, aesthetic trends and religious change. Most of the rose windows were replaced with clear glass (the stained glass was later restored) in the 18th century. Revolutionary anti-clericalism toppled countless statues and the spire was taken down between 1786 and 1792. Not least, Viollet-le-Duc, the fervent 19th-century

Clockwise from top left: Exterior of Notre-Dame; Notre-Dame at night, seen across the Seine; the soaring interior; the Rose Window from inside the cathedral; 19th-century carvings, replacements for statues destroyed during the Revolution; the Rose Window seen from outside the building

medievalist architect, was let loose on its restoration and initiated radical alterations.

Interior grandeur The hushed, softly lit stone interior contains numerous chapels, tombs and statues. The sacristy on the south side of the choir is where the treasure of Notre-Dame is kept: medieval manuscripts, religious paraphernalia and relics, including the Crown of Thorns. The Crypt is often overlooked because its entrance is outside, but you can see Roman foundations and archaeological finds down there. Climb the towers (387 steps; no elevator) for fantastic views and a close-up of the gargoyles. Look closely at the three asymmetrical sculpted portals on the facade: These once served as a Bible for illiterate worshippers. Finally, walk round the cathedral for a view of its extravagant flying buttresses.

THE BASICS

www.notredamedeparis.fr
J7
Place du Parvis Notre-Dame–Place Jean-Paul II, 75004
01 42 34 56 10. Crypt 01 55 42 50 10
Cathedral Mon–Fri 8–6.45, Sat, Sun 8–7.15. Towers Jul, Aug Mon–Fri 9–6.30, Sat, Sun 9am–11pm; Apr–Jun, Sep daily 10–6.30; Oct–Mar daily 10–5.30. Treasury Mon–Sat 9.30–6, Sun 1.30–6.30
Cité, Saint-Michel
21, 24, 38, 47, 85, 96
RER Lines B and C, Saint-Michel
Good (not in towers)
Cathedral free; charge for tower and treasury

Sainte-Chapelle

TOP 25

HIGHLIGHTS

- Rose window
- Oratory
- 10-year restoration, completed in 2009
- Tombs of canons
- Stained-glass depiction of Christ's Passion
- Saint Louis in the 'Story of the Relics' window

TIPS

- The upper chapel can become extremely crowded. The quietest times to visit are Tuesday and Friday morning.
- Pick up an information card near the exit.

Sainte-Chapelle's spire, soaring 75m (246ft) above the ground, is in itself a great expression of faith, but this is surpassed, inside, by the glowing intensity of the stained-glass windows reaching up to a star-studded roof, now spectacularly restored.

Masterpiece One of Paris's oldest and most significant monuments stands in the precincts of the Palais de Justice. The chapel was built by Louis IX (later canonized) to house relics he had acquired at exorbitant cost during the crusades, and which included what was reputed to be the Crown of Thorns, as well as fragments of the Cross and drops of Christ's blood (now kept in Notre-Dame). Pierre de Montreuil is believed to have masterminded this delicate Gothic construction, bypassing the use of

Clockwise from left: The intricate stained-glass Rose Window on the western wall of the upper chapel, representing the Apocalypse; looking up to the ceiling of the upper chapel; stained glass; the intricate carvings inside the upper chapel; the lower chapel

flying buttresses, incorporating a lower chapel for palace servants to worship in and installing more than 600sq m (6,458sq ft) of striking stained glass above. Completed in 1248 in record time, it was Louis IX's private chapel, with discreet access from what was then the royal palace.

Apocalypse More than 1,000 biblical scenes are illustrated in the 16 windows, starting with Genesis in the window to the left of the entrance, and working round the chapel to finish with the Apocalypse, in the rose window. The only non-biblical theme is in the final window, which tells how the holy relics came to Paris. Two-thirds of the windows are 13th-century originals, the oldest stained glass in Paris. The statues of the Apostles are mostly copies—the damaged originals are at the Musée National du Moyen-Âge (▷ 43).

THE BASICS

www.sainte-chapelle.monuments-nationaux.fr
J6
4 boulevard du Palais, Île de la Cité, 75001
01 53 40 60 97
Mar–end Oct 9.30–6; Nov–end Feb daily 9–5
Cité, Châtelet
21, 24, 38, 85, 96
RER Line B, St-Michel
Moderate (joint ticket with the Conciergerie expensive)
Guided tours by appointment only; tel 01 53 40 60 93

La Seine Boat Trip

TOP 25

THE BOAT TRIP

Distance: 11km (7 miles)
Allow: Just over 1 hour
Start/End: Square du Vert-Galant, Pont Neuf
How to get there:
Pont Neuf
24, 27, 58, 67, 70, 72, 74, 75
From the Métro station, walk over the Pont Neuf. About halfway across, on the right, is a sign for the Vedettes du Pont Neuf. Go down the steps to the square.

TIP

- Evening is a great time to go on this trip, when the monuments are lit up. Try to go when the weather is good so you can sit on deck and get the best views.

A river cruise along the Seine is a great way to view some of Paris's key sights from a different perspective. And in just over an hour you can see many of the famous landmarks.

Romantic trip The boat leaves from square du Vert-Galant and heads west. The first bridge is the pedestrian-only Pont des Arts, one of Paris's most romantic bridges. On the Right Bank you can see the Museé du Louvre (▷ 76–77). After passing under the Pont du Carrousel and the Pont Royal you'll see the Musée d'Orsay (▷ 26–27) on the Left Bank and then the 18th-century Palais Bourbon. On the Right Bank is place de la Concorde (▷ 80). The boat passes under the ornate Pont Alexandre III (▷ 33). On the Right Bank you can see the Grand Palais and Petit Palais and on the Left Bank, in the distance, is Les Invalides (▷ 24–25). After passing under the Pont des Invalides, the Pont de l'Alma and the Passerelle Debilly, the boat rounds a bend and you are greeted by a spectacular view of the Eiffel Tower (▷ 30–31) on the Left Bank. The Pont d'Iéna spans the river between the Eiffel Tower on

Passengers on a sightseeing trip along the Seine (left); a tour boat passing beneath the Pont Neuf (middle); looking along the Seine at the Île Saint-Louis (right)

the Left Bank and the Jardins du Trocadéro on the Right Bank. The boat passes under this bridge before turning and heading back in the opposite direction to the Île de la Cité. You'll see the cupola of the Institut de France on the right before you pass under the southern side of the Pont Neuf. The next two bridges are the Pont Saint-Michel, leading to the Latin Quarter and the Sorbonne university, and the Petit Pont, the smallest bridge in Paris. On the Île de la Cité you can see the beautiful Notre-Dame cathedral (▷ 44–45).

Bridges Several bridges farther along, to your right, is the Institut du Monde Arabe (▷ 51) and the outdoor sculptures of the Musée de la Sculpture en Plein Air. The boat circles around the picturesque Île Saint-Louis (▷ 51). After three more bridges you can see Paris's town hall, the Hôtel de Ville, on the Right Bank. As the boat sails back along the other side of the Île de la Cité, you'll pass the city's oldest hospital, the Hôtel-Dieu, and the Conciergerie (▷ 40–41). Look for the 16th-century clock, the Tour de l'Horloge, on the facade of the Conciergerie. The boat passes back under the Pont Neuf and the cruise ends where it began.

THE BASICS

www.vedettesdupontneuf.com

☎ 01 46 33 98 38

Mar–end Oct daily 10, 11.15, 12 and every half-hour from 1.30 to 7, then 8, 9, 9.30, 10 and 10.30; rest of year Mon–Thu 10.30, 11.15, 12, 2, 2.45, 3.30, 4.15, 5, 5.45, 6.30, 8 and 10, Fri–Sun 10.30, 11.15, 12, 2, 2.45, 3.30, 4.15, 5, 5.45, 6.30, 8, 9, 9.45, 10.30. Times may vary

Expensive

? Pick up a free route map from the boarding platform

More to See

ARÈNES DE LUTÈCE

A partly ruined Gallo-Roman amphitheatre now popular with boules-players and teenagers. Destroyed in AD285, it was restored in the 1910s.

K8 4 rue des Arènes Daylight hours Jussieu, Cardinal Lemoine

BIBLIOTHÉQUE NATIONALE DE FRANCE–FRANÇOIS MITTERRAND

www.bnf.fr

Around 13 million books and documents are owned by the BNF. The modern library, with its glass corner towers designed like four open books, is on the east edge of the Left Bank.

Off map at M9 Quai François-Mauriac, 75013 01 53 79 59 59 Upper Garden reading rooms Mon 2–7, Tue–Sat 9–7, Sun 1–7 Bibliotheque François-Mitterrand

CAFÉ LES DEUX MAGOTS

www.lesdeuxmagots.fr

Some 25 whisky brands, a good mix of tourists and the literary shades of Truman Capote and Hemingway. It's also a strategic spot for street artists.

G7 170 boulevard Saint-Germain/ 6 place Saint-Germain-des-Prés 75006 01 45 48 55 25 Daily 7.30am–1am Saint-Germain-des-Prés

CAFÉ DE FLORE

www.cafe-de-flore.com

Haunted by ghosts of existentialists Sartre and de Beauvoir, who held court here during the Occupation, this café is pricey but a good spot for people-watching.

G7 172 boulevard Saint-Germain, 75006 01 45 48 55 26 Daily 7.30am–1.30am Saint-Germain-des-Prés

ÉGLISE SAINT-ÉTIENNE-DU-MONT

Dating from the 15th century, this church has a bizarre combination of Gothic, Renaissance and classical architecture. The unique wood screen arching over the nave is a highlight, with its delicate fretwork.

J8 Place Sainte-Genevieve, 75005 Mon 2.30–7, Tue–Sat 8.45–7.30, Sun 8.45–12, 2.30–7.30 Cardinal Lemoine

Relaxing at Café de Flore

Arènes de Lutèce

ÉGLISE SAINT-GERMAIN-DES-PRÉS

www.eglise-sgp.org

Paris's oldest church dates from the 11th century; it preserves 12th-century flying buttresses, an original tower and the choir. There are organ recitals.

G6 · Place Saint-Germain-des-Prés, 75006 · Daily 9–7 · Saint-Germain-des-Prés, Odéon

ÉGLISE SAINT-SÉVERIN

www.saint-severin.com

Built from the 13th to 16th centuries on the site of an 11th-century church. Inside is a double ambulatory, palm-tree vaulting and lovely stained glass.

J7 · 1 rue des Prêtres Saint-Séverin, 75005 · Mon–Sat 11–7, Sun 9–8.30 · Saint-Michel

ÉGLISE SAINT-SULPICE

www.paroisse-saint-sulpice-paris.org

Work started in 1646, ending 134 years later with asymmetrical towers and mixed styles. Note Delacroix's murals in the first chapel on the right and the famous organs.

G7 · Place Saint-Sulpice, 75006 · Daily 7.30–7.30 · Saint-Sulpice

ÎLE SAINT-LOUIS

The Île Saint-Louis maintains a spirit of its own. Rue Saint-Louis-en-l'Île is lined with art shops and restaurants.

K/L7 · Pont Marie, Sully Morland

INSTITUT DU MONDE ARABE

www.imarabe.org

Clean lines, aluminium walls and glass are the hallmarks here. The museum has fine metalwork, ceramics, textiles, carpets and calligraphy.

K7 · 1 rue des Fossés Saint-Bernard, 75005 · 01 40 51 38 38; 01 40 51 38 11 · Tue–Sun 10–6. Library Tue–Sat 1–8 · Cardinal Lemoine, Jussieu

MÉMORIAL DES MARTYRS DE LA DÉPORTATION

A stark crypt lined with 200,000 quartz pebbles commemorates French citizens deported by the Nazis.

K7 · Square de l'Île de France, 75004 · 01 46 33 87 56 · Apr–end Oct daily 10–12, 2–7; Nov–end Mar 10–12, 2–5 · Cité

Looking through the aluminium-and-glass facade at the Institut du Monde Arabe

MUSÉUM NATIONAL D'HISTOIRE NATURELLE

www.mnhn.fr

In one of Paris's prettiest parks, this museum's spectacular displays cover everything from the evolution of the living world to endangered species. Don't miss the tropical greenhouses.

K9 57 rue Cuvier, 75005 01 40 79 30 00 Grande Galerie de l'Evolution Wed–Mon 10–6. Paleontology and Mineralogy Wed–Mon 10–5 Place Monge, Gare d'Austerlitz Prices vary

NO. 26 RUE VAVIN

This striking 1912 building is faced in blue-and-white ceramic and has stepped balconies.

G8 26 rue Vavin, 75006 Vavin

PONT MARIE

This bridge, built in 1635 and restored in 1850, was once lined with four-storey houses—some were later partly destroyed by floods and others were demolished in 1788.

K7 Pont Marie, Quai des Célestins

PONT NEUF

Dating from 1604, Paris's oldest bridge ironically bears the name of 'New Bridge'. The houseless design was highly controversial at the time.

H6 Pont Neuf, Île de la Cité

RUE DU CHERCHE-MIDI

César's sculpture on the rue de Sèvres crossroads marks out this typical Left Bank street, home to the famous Poîlane bakery (No. 8) and the Musée Hébert (No. 85).

G7 Saint-Sulpice

RUE JACOB

Antiques and interior-decoration shops monopolize this picturesque stretch. Make a 20-pace detour to the Musée Delacroix on the rue de Furstemberg.

G6 Saint-Germain-des-Prés

SQUARE DU VERT-GALANT

Enjoy a quintessential view of bridges and the Louvre in this tiny, pretty park.

H6 Place du Pont-Neuf, 75001 Apr–end Sep daily 9am–10.30pm; Oct–end Mar daily 9–7 Pont Neuf

A boat passes under the Pont Neuf

The famous Boulangerie Poîlane

Quartier Latin Walk

Soak up the medieval atmosphere of the picturesque Latin Quarter as you walk the narrow streets where Dante once taught outside.

DISTANCE: 2.5km (1.5 miles) **ALLOW:** 1 hour

START

PLACE SAINT-MICHEL
Saint-Michel 21, 24, 27, 38, 85, 96

1. Start at place Saint-Michel and walk across to the Fontaine Saint-Michel. Cross boulevard Saint-Michel and walk down the medieval rue de la Huchette. Cross over rue de Petit Pont.

2. Turn left, then immediately right into rue de la Bûcherie, with its views of Notre-Dame. Continue to square René Viviani, where you can linger for a while.

3. Leave the square near the church of Saint-Julien-le-Pauvre. From the church, follow the road to the right to rue Saint-Jacques. Cross and walk down rue Saint-Séverin to rue de la Harpe.

4. Rue de la Harpe, to the left, leads to boulevard Saint-Germain. Cross the boulevard to the garden of the Musée National du Moyen-Âge.

5. Take boulevard Saint-Germain back to boulevard Saint-Michel, then turn left.

6. Walk up boulevard Saint-Michel, then turn right onto rue de l'École de Médecine. Turn left onto rue André Dubois, then up steps to rue Monsieur le Prince. Turn left onto this road, with its shops and inexpensive restaurants.

7. Just before Polidor, turn right into rue Racine and continue to place de l'Odéon. Turn right on rue de l'Odéon to reach Carrefour de l'Odéon. Continue to boulevard Saint-Germain. Cross and go down rue de l'Ancienne Comédie.

8. At the Buci crossroads turn sharp right onto rue Saint-André des Arts. This leads back to place Saint-Michel, where you can relax in a café.

END

PLACE SAINT-MICHEL
Saint-Michel 21, 24, 27, 38, 85, 96

Shopping

DYPTIQUE
The ultimate in beautifully crafted candles, in a choice of 48 exquisite scents. There's also a divine range of eaux de cologne.
J7 34 boulevard Saint-Germain, 75005 01 43 26 45 27 Mon–Sat 10–7 Maubert-Mutualité

GALERIE DOCUMENTS
Original posters and etchings from 1890 to 1940 by such masters as Toulouse-Lautrec and Alphonse Mucha.
H6 53 rue de Seine, 75006 01 43 54 50 68 Tue–Sat 10.30–7, Mon 2.30–7 Odéon, Mabillon

LA HUNE
This excellent literary bookshop has an extensive art and architecture section. It's great for late-night browsing as it stays open until nearly midnight.
G6 170 boulevard Saint-Germain, 75006 01 45 48 35 85 Mon–Sat 10am–11.45pm, Sun 11–7.45 Saint-Germain-des-Prés

LOLLIPOPS
A boho-chic collection of bags, scarves, hats and jewellery. Products are displayed by colour, making it easy to find coordinating pieces.
G7 48 rue du Four, 75006 01 42 84 25 15 Mon–Sat 10.30–7 Saint-Sulpice, Saint-Germain-des-Prés

MARCHÉ AUX FLEURS
Flower and plant market, with everything you can imagine.
J6 Place Louis Lépine, 75004, Île de la Cité Mon–Sat 8–7.30 (bird market on Sun) Cité

MARIAGE FRÈRES
This Parisian institution sells 600 teas from around the world and has a chic tea room. The original store is in rue du Bourg-Tibourg (▷ 68).
H6 13 rue des Grands-Augustins, 75006 01 40 51 82 50 Daily 10.30–7.30; tea room 12–7 Odéon

MARIE MERCIÉ
Extravagant hats for women, from classic to theatrical. The men's equivalent store, Anthony Peto, is at 56 rue Tiquetonne, 75002.
H7 23 rue Saint-Sulpice, 75006 01 43 26 45 83 Mon–Sat 11–7 Odéon

WINDOW-SHOPPING

Some Parisian streets do not fit any convenient label and so make for intriguing window-shopping. Try rue Jean-Jacques Rousseau and Passage Véro-Dodat, rue Saint-Roch, rue Monsieur-le-Prince and parallel rue de l'Odéon, rue Saint-Sulpice, rue des Francs-Bourgeois and rue du Pont-Louis-Philippe or rue de la Roquette. For luxury goods, take a stroll along the rue du Faubourg-Saint-Honoré.

PIERRE HERMÉ
Pierre Hermé's couture pastries are as visually stunning as they are mouthwatering. His gold-leaf ornamented chocolate cake is legendary.
G7 72 rue Bonaparte, 75006 01 43 54 47 77 Mon–Fri, Sun 9–7, Sat 9–7.30 Saint-Sulpice, Mabillon

RUE MOUFFETARD
A tourist classic straggling down a winding, narrow, hilly street, with a wonderful array of shops and stalls selling fruit and veg, aromatic cheeses and charcuteries. Good café stops en route.
J9 Rue Mouffetard, 75005 Daily Monge

SHAKESPEARE AND COMPANY
A charming English bookshop that stocks new and used books. There is also a small library upstairs.
J7 37 rue de la Bûcherie, 75005 01 43 25 40 93 Mon–Sat 10am–11pm, Sun 11–11 Saint-Michel

SONIA RYKIEL
Ready-to-wear fashion house with ranges of accessories and perfumes.
G6 175 boulevard Saint-Germain, 75006 01 49 54 60 60 Mon–Sat 10.30–7 Saint-Germain-des-Prés, Sèvres-Babylone

Entertainment and Nightlife

LA BALLE AU BOND

www.laballeaubond.fr

A floating concert and theatre venue with a lively ambience. The setting on the Seine couldn't be more spectacular. There's a separate restaurant on board. See website for schedule.

G6, K7 Apr–end Oct, 3 quai Malaquais, near Pont des Arts; Nov–end Mar, quai de la Tournelle, near Notre-Dame cathedral 01 40 46 85 12 Pont Neuf (summer) or Maubert-Mutualité (winter)

CAVEAU DE LA HUCHETTE

www.caveaudelahuchette.fr

Still going strong after 60 years, a basement bar with dancing and live jazz from 9.30pm onwards.

J7 5 rue de la Huchette, 75005 01 43 26 65 05 Saint-Michel

LE CHAMPO

Come here for cult classics. Retrospectives explore the work of directors such as the Marx Brothers, Claude Chabrol and Jacques Tati. Films are in the original language.

J7 51 rue des Écoles, 75005 01 43 54 51 60 Daily 1.50–10 Saint-Michel, Odéon, Cluny-La Sorbonne

LUCERNAIRE/ CENTRE NATIONAL D'ART ET D'ESSAI

www.lucernaire.fr

A complex of three cinemas, an art gallery, bar, restaurant and three theatres staging a wide variety of plays.

G8 53 rue Notre-Dame-des-Champs, 75006 01 45 44 57 34 Vavin, Notre-Dame-des-Champs

MUSÉE NATIONAL DU MOYEN-ÂGE

www.musee-moyenage.fr

This medieval mansion is home to a museum (▷ 43), but it also hosts classical and chamber music concerts.

J7 6 place Paul-Painlevé, 75005 01 53 73 78 16 Wed–Mon 9.15–5.45; free concerts of medieval music: Fri 12.30pm, Sat 4pm Cluny–La Sorbonne

STUDIO GALANDE

Cult movie *The Rocky Horror Picture Show* is shown here every Friday and Saturday at 10.10pm—come dressed up if you like. The rest of the week screenings vary from art films to cartoons.

J7 42 rue Galande, 75005 01 43 54 72 71 Saint-Michel, Maubert-Mutualité, Cluny

CONCERTS

Numerous classical music concerts are held in churches—try Saint-Eustache, Saint-Germain-des-Prés, Saint-Julien-le-Pauvre, Saint-Louis-en-l'Île, Saint-Roch and Saint-Séverin (www.ampconcerts.com). Seats are reasonably priced and the quality of music is sometimes very high. May to September free concerts are held in parks. Schedules are available at the Office du Tourisme or the Hôtel de Ville.

THÉÂTRE DE LA HUCHETTE

www.theatrehuchette.com

Two of Ionesco's masterpieces, *La Cantatrice Chauve* (*The Bald Soprano*) and *La Leçon* (*The Lesson*), have been performed here six days a week for over 50 years.

J7 23 rue de la Huchette, 75005 01 43 26 38 99 Saint-Michel

THÉÂTRE DE NESLE

www.galeriedenesle.com

Small Left Bank theatre in the vaulted basement of a 17th-century mansion. Occasional English-language plays and regular shows for kids (in French).

H6 8 rue de Nesle, 75006 01 46 34 61 04 Odéon, Pont Neuf

WAGG

www.wagg.fr

More intimate than most clubs, the smaller dance floor gives this venue a welcoming atmosphere. The house, funk, disco, dance and salsa music draws a cool mid-20s to mid-30s crowd.

H7 62 rue Mazarine, 75006 01 55 42 22 01 Fri, Sat 9.30pm–dawn, Sun 3–5 (Salsa class), 5–midnight Saint-Germain-des-Prés, Odéon

Restaurants

PRICES

Prices are approximate, based on a 3-course meal for one person.

€€€	over €90
€€	€30–€90
€	under €30

ALCAZAR (€€)

English designer Terence Conran's bar-cum-restaurant offers some of the best fish in town. The lounge bar upstairs has international DJs.

H6 62 rue Mazarine, 75006 01 53 10 19 99 Daily lunch, dinner Odéon

LE COMPTOIR (€€)

This gastro-bistro, under the expert eye of chef Yves Camdeborde, champions modern French cuisine. Reservations are not taken for lunch, but reserve ahead for dinner.

H7 Hôtel Relais Saint-Germain, 9 carrefour de l'Odéon, 75006 01 44 22 07 97 Daily lunch, dinner Odéon

LA COUPOLE (€€)

An institution since the 1920s. Go for the historic setting rather than the food.

F9 102 boulevard du Montparnasse, 75014 01 43 20 14 20 Daily 8am–1am Vavin

JACQUES CAGNA (€€€)

Chef Jacques Cagna has been reinventing French classics for decades. Expect delicacies in an elegant setting.

H6 14 rue des Grands-Augustins, 75006 01 43 26 49 39 Tue–Fri lunch, dinner, Mon, Sat dinner Saint-Michel, Odéon

KITCHEN GALERIE BIS (€€)

In the former home of Picasso and Balzac, this new designer restaurant is from the same stable as Ze Kitchen Galerie (▷ below). Expect fresh, natural cuisine with Asian accents.

H6 25 rue des Grands-Augustins, 75006 01 46 33 00 85 Tue–Sat lunch, dinner Odéon

LOUIS VINS (€€)

Large restaurant with quirky yet homey decor, lively ambience and excellent value.

J7 9 rue de la Montaigne-Sainte-Geneviève, 75005 01 43 29 12 12 Daily lunch, dinner Maubert-Mutualité

LA COUPOLE

Horror struck Parisian hearts in the mid-1980s when it was announced that La Coupole had been bought by property developers and several floors were to be added on top. This happened, but the famous old murals (by Juan Gris, Soutine, Chagall, Delaunay and many more) have been reinstated, the red-velvet seats preserved and the art deco lights duly restored. The 1920s interior is now a historic monument.

LE PETIT SAINT-BENOÎT (€)

Popular, inexpensive old classic; decor barely changed since the 1930s.

G6 4 rue Saint-Benoît, 75006 01 42 60 27 92 Mon–Sat lunch, dinner Saint-Germain-des-Prés

LA TOUR D'ARGENT (€€€)

Historic restaurant best known for duck. Fabulous view, and great wine cellar. It has been demoted to one Michelin star, but is still superb.

K7 15–17 quai de la Tournelle, 75005 (facing Île Saint-Louis) 01 43 54 23 31 Tue–Sun lunch, dinner Pont-Marie, Cardinal Lemoine

YUGARAJ (€€)

One of the best Indian restaurants, discreet and elegant. Traditional curries plus surprising dishes.

H6 14 rue Dauphine, 75006 01 43 26 44 91 Tue, Wed, Fri–Sun lunch, dinner, Thu dinner Pont Neuf, Odeon

ZE KITCHEN GALERIE (€€)

Chic restaurant with an elegant modern interior and inventive cuisine.

H6 4 rue des Grands-Augustins, 75006 01 44 32 00 32 Mon–Fri lunch, dinner, Sat dinner Saint-Michel

The Marais was home to the aristocracy before becoming a slum. This now beautiful, vibrant quarter is the heart of the Jewish and gay communities. The lively Bastille area has a more commercial feel.

3
4
5
6
7
H
J
K
LES HALLES
Saint-Eustache
Les Halles
Jardin du Forum des Halles
Forum des Halles
Châtelet Les Halles (+RER)
Fontaine des Innocents
Centre Georges Pompidou
Café Beaubourg
IRCAM
Saint-Merri
Hôtel de Ville
Hôtel de Ville (RER)
Sentier
Réaumur Sébastopol
Étienne Marcel (RER)
Rambuteau
Louvre-Rivoli
Châtelet
Pont Neuf-La Monnaie
Saint-Germain-l'Auxerrois
RUE RÉAUMUR
RUE ÉTIENNE MARCEL
RUE J-J ROUSSEAU
BOULEVARD DE SÉBASTOPOL
RUE DE TURBIGO
RUE BEAUBOURG
RUE DU RENARD
RUE DE RIVOLI
QUAI DU LOUVRE
QUAI DE LA MÉGISSERIE
QUAI DE GESVRES
QUAI DE L'HOTEL DE VILLE
AVENUE VICTORIA
PONT NEUF
PONT AU CHANGE
PONT NOTRE-DAME
Pont L Philippe
Seine
Rue Montmartre
Rue Montorgueil
Rue Saint-Denis
Rue Saint-Martin
Rue Rambuteau
Rue Berger
Rue Saint-Honoré
Rue du Louvre
Rue Coquillière
Rue Tiquetonne
Rue Greneta
Rue Saint-Sauveur
Rue Mandar
Rue Bachaumont
Rue d'Argout
Rue Léopold Bellan
Rue du Caire
Rue Palestro
Rue Papin
Rue Marie Stuart
Pass du Grand Cerf
Rue du Jour
Rue aux Ours
Rue Quincampoix
Rue Brantôme
R Michel
Rue Baillеul
Rue Perrault
Rue du Roule
Rue du Pont Neuf
Rue de la Monnaie
R des Bourdonnais
R B Poirée
R des Orfèvres
Rue Saint-Germain-l'Auxerrois
Rue Jean Lantier
R des Innocents
Rue de la Ferronnerie
Rue des Halles
Rue des Lombards
Rue Pernelle
Rue Brisemiche
Rue Saint-Merri
R G Langevin
Rue S le Franc
Rue du Temple
Rue de la Verrerie
Rue de Lobau
R de Brosse
Rue du Plâtre
Rue Sainte-Croix
Pl du Louvre
Musée des Arts et Métiers
Musée d'Art et d'Histoire du Judaïsme
0
250 m
250 yds

Musée Picasso
Rue Vieille du Temple
Musée Cognacq-Jay
Rue des Rosiers
Musée Carnavalet
Place des Vosges
Hôtel de Sully
Maison de Victor Hugo
Maison Européenne de la Photographie
Pavillon de l'Arsenal
Musée de la Chasse et de la Nature
Musée de l'Histoire de France
Synagogue
Saint-Sébastien-Froissart
Chemin Vert
Bréguet Sabin
Bastille
Saint-Paul-Le Marais
Sully Morland
Opéra Bastille
LE MARAIS
BASTILLE
PLACE DE LA BASTILLE
RUE DU TEMPLE
RUE DE TURBIGO
RÉAUMUR
RUE DE RIVOLI
RUE SAINT-ANTOINE
BOULEVARD BEAUMARCHAIS
BOULEVARD RICHARD LENOIR
BOULEVARD HENRI IV
BOULEVARD BOURDON
BOULEVARD MORLAND
QUAI DES CÉLESTINS
QUAI HENRI IV
Canal Saint Martin
Rue de Turenne
Rue Froissart
Rue Saint-Claude
Rue Saint-Gilles
Rue des Minimes
Rue des Francs-Bourgeois
Rue de Sévigné
Rue Payenne
Rue Elzévir
Rue du Parc Royal
Rue de Thorigny
Rue de Bretagne
Rue Charlot
Rue de Saintonge
Rue du Poitou
Rue des Archives
Rue Pastourelle
Rue des Quatre Fils
Rue Barbette
Rue Pavée
Rue Malher
Rue de Jarente
Rue d'Ormesson
Rue Charlemagne
Rue Saint-Paul
Rue Neuve Saint-Pierre
Rue Beautreillis
Rue Castex
Rue de Sully
Rue de l'Arsenal
Rue des Tournelles
Rue Amelot
Rue Saint-Sabin
Rue Scarron
Rue du Chemin Vert
Rue de Hesse
Rue des Arquebusiers
Rue Commines
R de Normandie
R Debelleyme
R de Beauce
Rue Portefoin
Rue Vertbois
Rue Volta
Rue Dupetit-Thouars
Rue de la Corderie
Rue de Picardie
Rue Perrée
Rue Caffarelli
Rue E. Spuller
Rue P. Dubois
Rue G. Vicaire
R de la Perle
Rue du Roi de Sicile
Rue des Ecouffes
R F Duval
Rue du Trésor
Rue Miron
Rue du Figuier
R du Fauconnier
Rue des Jardins Saint-Paul
Rue Charles V
Rue des Lions Saint-Paul
Rue du Petit Musc
R J Cousin
R de la Cerisaie
Rue J Coeur
Rue de Lesdiguières
Rue de la Bastille
Impasse J Beausire
R J Beausire
R de Birague
R Roger Verlomme
Rue du Foin
R Agrippa d'Aubigné
L
M

Centre Georges Pompidou

HIGHLIGHTS

- Design by Richard Rogers, Renzo Piano and Jean-François Bodin
- View from the escalator
- Stravinsky fountain
- Trendy and cool design in Georges restaurant
- Avant-premières of new films and retrospectives of the work of famed directors in the cinema
- Design shop on mezzanine

TIP

- The official guidebook has information about 150 of the exhibits and is worth buying before you visit the Museum of Modern Art.

Late opening hours make an exhibition visit possible between an aperitif and dinner in this still-controversial cultural area. You can take your pick between the genesis of modernism, an art film or a drama performance.

High-tech culture More than a mere landmark in the extensive facelift that Paris has undergone since the 1970s, the high-tech Centre Pompidou (known to Parisians as Beaubourg) is a hive of changing cultural activity. Contemporary art, architecture, design, photography, theatre, cinema and dance are all represented, while the lofty structure offers exceptional views over central Paris. Take the transparent escalator tubes for a bird's-eye view of the piazza, where jugglers, artists, musicians and portrait artists perform for the crowds.

Clockwise from top left: Futuristic features on the exterior of the building; the inside-out exterior; the Stravinsky Fountain at place Igor Stravinsky; inside the Forum; detail of a sculpture in the Stravinsky fountain

Facelift The Centre Pompidou was completely renovated for the new millennium. The permanent collections of the Musée National d'Art Moderne feature work from 1905 to 1960 on the fifth floor and 1960 to the present on the fourth floor. Items from the 59,000-strong collection are changed regularly and range from Cubism by Georges Braque to Pop Art by Andy Warhol and video art by Korean artist Nam June Paik. For a chronological overview start on the fifth floor. Levels 1 and 6 are for temporary exhibitions, while a public information library is on levels 1, 2 and 3. The ground level includes a bookshop (there are other boutiques on levels 1, 4 and 6), a post office and a children's workshop. There are cinemas on the first and lower floors and the restaurant Georges, with its wonderful views over the city, is on the top floor.

THE BASICS

www.centrepompidou.fr
K5
Place Georges-Pompidou, 75004
01 44 78 12 33
Museum and exhibits Wed–Mon 11–9; Atelier Brancusi (▷ 17) Wed–Mon 2–6; Library Mon, Wed–Fri 12–10, Sat, Sun 11–10
Georges restaurant on 6th floor (▷ 70); café on mezzanine
Rambuteau, Hôtel de Ville
38, 47, 67, 75, 76
RER Line A, B, Châtelet-Les Halles
Excellent
Moderate

Musée Carnavalet

Inside the museum (left) and the ivy-clad exterior (right)

THE BASICS

www.carnavalet.paris.fr
L6
23 rue de Sévigné, 75003
01 44 59 58 58
Tue–Sun 10–6
Saint-Paul
29, 69, 76, 96
Carnavalet: few; Le Peletier: good
Free; temporary exhibitions moderate

HIGHLIGHTS

- Statue of Louis XIV
- Le Brun's ceiling painting
- *Destruction of the Bastille*, Hubert Robert
- Bastille prison keys
- Le Sueur's comic strip
- Proust's bedroom
- Ballroom from Hôtel de Wendel
- Napoleon's picnic case
- Archaeological collection in the Orangerie
- Formal garden in La Cour de la Victoire
- Robespierre's last letter

There is no better museum than this to plunge you into the history of Paris, and its renovated mansion setting is hard to beat. Period rooms, objects, documents and paintings combine to illustrate the city's turbulent past.

Ornamental excess This captivating collection is displayed within adjoining 16th- and 17th-century town houses. The main entrance is through the superb courtyard of the Hôtel Carnavalet (1548), once home of the celebrated writer Madame de Sévigné. Here attention focuses on the Roman period, the Middle Ages, the Renaissance and the decorative excess reached under Louis XIV, Louis XV and Louis XVI. Some of the richly painted and sculpted interiors are original to the building; others, such as the wood panels from the Hôtel Colbert de Villacerf and Brunetti's trompe-l'œil staircase paintings, have been brought in.

Revolution to the present Next door, the well-renovated Hôtel Le Peletier de Saint-Fargeau (1688) exhibits remarkable objects from the Revolution—a period when anything and everything was emblazoned with slogans—and continues with Napoleon I's reign, the Restoration, the Second Empire, the Commune and finally the Belle Époque. Figures such as Robespierre and Madame de Récamier come to life within their chronological context. The collection ends in the early 20th century with remarkable reconstructions of interiors, and paintings by Maurice Utrillo, Paul Signac, Albert Marquet and Léonard Foujita.

Housing surrounding place des Vosges (left); a café on the square (right)

Place des Vosges

Paris's oldest and best-preserved square connects the quarters of the Marais and the Bastille. You can marvel at its architectural unity and stroll under its arcades, now animated by outdoor restaurants and window-shoppers.

Place Royale Ever since the square was inaugurated in 1612 with a spectacular fireworks display, countless luminaries have chosen to live in the redbrick houses overlooking the central garden of plane trees. Before that, the square was the site of a royal palace, the Hôtel des Tournelles (1388), which was later abandoned and demolished by Catherine de Médicis in 1559, when her husband Henri II died there. The arcaded facades were commissioned by Henri IV, who incorporated two royal pavilions at the heart of the north and south sides of the square and named it Place Royale.

Celebrities After the Revolution the square was renamed place des Vosges in tribute to the first French district to pay its new taxes. The first example of planned development in the history of Paris, these 36 town houses (nine on each side and still intact), with their steep-pitched roofs, surround a formal garden laid out with gravel paths and fountains. The symmetry of the houses has always attracted a string of celebrities, including princesses, official mistresses, Cardinal Richelieu, Victor Hugo (his house is now a museum) and Théophile Gautier. Smart shops and chic art galleries, with prices to match and ideal for window-shopping, line its arcades.

THE BASICS

www.musee-hugo.paris.fr
M6
Place des Vosges, 75004
Several, including Café Hugo at No. 22
Bastille, Chemin Vert, Saint-Paul
29, 96
Good
Free

HIGHLIGHTS

- Pavillon du Roi
- Pavillon de la Reine
- Statue of Louis XIII
- No. 6, Maison de Victor Hugo
- No. 21, residence of Cardinal Richelieu
- Door knockers
- *Trompe-l'œil* bricks
- Four matching fountains

More to See

CAFÉ BEAUBOURG

Opposite the Pompidou Centre, preferred by artists, critics and book-reading poseurs. Discreet tables in a spacious setting designed by Christian de Portzamparc.

K5 · 43 rue Saint-Merri, 75004 · 01 48 87 63 96 · Sun–Thu 8am–1am, Fri, Sat 8am–2am · Hôtel de Ville, Chatelet, Rambuteau

ÉGLISE SAINT-EUSTACHE

www.saint-eustache.org

Renaissance in detail and decoration but Gothic in general design. Frequent organ recitals.

J4 · 2 rue du Jour/place du Jour, 75001 · Les Halles

ÉGLISE SAINT-MERRI

Superb example of Flamboyant Gothic, though not completed until 1612. Renaissance stained glass, murals, impressive organ loft and Paris's oldest church bell (1331). Regular concerts.

K5 · 78 rue Saint-Martin, 75004 · 01 42 71 40 75 for concert information · Hôtel de Ville

MAISON EUROPÉENNE DE LA PHOTOGRAPHIE

www.mep-fr.org

A stylish complex for contemporary photography, with dynamic temporary shows. The galleries spread over five floors of the 18th-century Hôtel Hénault de Cantobre, and a new wing.

L6 · 5–7 rue de Fourcy, 75004 · 01 44 78 75 00 · Wed–Sun 11am–8pm · Saint-Paul · Moderate

MUSÉE COGNACQ-JAY

www.cognacq-jay.paris.fr

In a mansion furnished in 18th-century style, see the 18th-century paintings and objets d'art collected by Ernest Cognacq and his wife Louise Jay, founders of the La Samaritaine store.

L6 · Hôtel Donon, 8 rue Elzévir, 75003 · 01 40 27 07 21 · Tue–Sun 10–6 · Saint-Paul · Free

MUSÉE D'ART ET D'HISTOIRE DU JUDAÏSME

www.mahj.org

Jewish art and culture from medieval times to the present day, concentrating

Sophisticated Café Beaubourg

Église Sainte-Eustache

mainly on France but also including the rest of Europe and North Africa. Exhibits range from wedding items to works by Jewish artists such as Modigliani and Chagall.
K5 Hôtel de Saint-Aignan, 71 rue du Temple, 75003 01 53 01 86 60 Mon–Fri 11–6, Sun 10–6 Rambuteau, Hôtel de Ville Moderate

MUSÉE DES ARTS ET MÉTIERS

www.arts-et-metiers.net
Art meets science through antique clocks, optics, underwater items including a diving suit, vintage cars and mechanical toys.
K4 60 rue Réaumur, 75003 01 53 01 82 00 Tue–Sun 10–6 (Thu until 9.30pm) Arts et Métiers, Réaumur-Sébastopol Moderate

MUSÉE PICASSO

www.musee-picasso.fr
Massive collection of Picasso's paintings, sculptures, drawings and ceramics in a 17th-century mansion (currently closed for renovation). The fixtures are by Diego Giacometti, and some of the works are by Picasso's contemporaries.
L5 Hôtel Salé, 5 rue de Thorigny, 75003 01 42 71 25 21 Closed for renovation until 2012 Saint-Paul Moderate, free first Sun of month

PAVILLON DE L'ARSENAL

www.pavillon-arsenal.com
This strikingly designed building houses well-conceived exhibitions on urban Paris, alongside a display on the city's architectural evolution.
L7 21 boulevard Morland, 75004 01 42 76 33 97 Tue–Sat 10.30–6.30, Sun 11–7 Sully Morland Free

RUE DES ROSIERS

Effervescent street at the heart of Paris's Jewish quarter. Kosher butchers and restaurants, Hebrew bookshops and designer boutiques.
L6 Saint-Paul

RUE VIEILLE-DU-TEMPLE

The pulse of the hip Marais district, dense in bars, cafés and boutiques.
K6–L5 Saint-Paul

A shop on rue des Rosiers, in the Marais

Inside the Musée Picasso

Le Marais to the place des Vosges

The mansions of the Marais, where the rich and famous of the Renaissance era lived, are now mostly museums and monuments.

DISTANCE: 3km (2 miles) **ALLOW:** 1 hour

START

PLACE GEORGES-POMPIDOU (▷ 60–61)
Rambuteau, Hôtel du Ville

❶ After breakfast at Café Beaubourg (▷ 64) walk across place Georges-Pompidou in front of the museum and turn right onto rue Rambuteau, a lively food-shopping street.

❷ Turn left up rue des Archives, with the magnificent turreted Porte Clisson (1380) rising from the Hôtel de Soubise (1553–1704) on your right.

❸ Continue past a monumental fountain (1765) on your left and the 1651 Hôtel Guénégaud, which houses the Musée de la Chasse, diagonally opposite.

❹ Keep walking until you reach rue de Bretagne, turn right, enter the picturesque food and flower market of Les Enfants Rouges (closed Mon), then exit onto rue Charlot.

❺ Walk south to rue des Quatre-Fils. Turn left and go to rue Vieille-du-Temple (▷ 65).

❻ Note the garden of the Hôtel Salé, home to the Musée Picasso (▷ 65; closed for renovation until 2012), a short detour to your left, then continue to rue du Parc-Royal, where a small garden is overlooked by a row of restored 17th-century mansions.

❼ Take a detour to the right to look at the Hôtel de Chatillon. Continue to rue de Sévigné and go right. Admire the Musée Carnavalet (▷ 62), then continue, turning left on rue Sarento, then first right to the place du Marché Sainte-Catherine.

❽ South of the square, go left on rue Saint-Antoine and left again on rue de Birague. Continue to place des Vosges.

END

PLACE DES VOSGES (▷ 63)
Chemin Vert

Shopping

AGNÈS B
Agnès B's fashion is the epitome of young Parisian chic. Sharply cut clothes with original details.
J4 6 rue du Jour, 75001 01 45 08 56 56 Mon–Sat 10–7.30 Les Halles

ANTIK BATIK
The place to shop for ethnic-chic fashions, including embroidered blouses, batik-printed stoles and lingerie.
L6 18 rue de Turenne, 75004 01 44 78 02 00 Tue–Sat 11–7, Sun, Mon 2–7 Hôtel de Ville

ARTAZART
On the banks of the Canal Saint-Martin, this bookshop specializes in design, architecture, photography and fashion. A small gallery shows work by up-and-coming artists.
M7 83 quai de Valmy, 75010 01 40 40 24 00 Mon–Fri 10.30–7.30, Sat, Sun 2–8 Jacques Bonsergent, République

AZZEDINE ALAÏA
Silhouette-hugging dresses by an artistic genius of the fashion world.
K6 7 rue de Moussy, 75004 01 42 72 19 19 Mon–Sat 10–7 Hôtel de Ville

BHV
You can't buy shoes in this department store, but otherwise it's famous for having everything you'll ever need, from baby clothes to an electrical transformer.
K6 55 rue de la Verrerie, 75004 01 42 74 90 00 Mon, Tue, Thu, Fri 9.30–7.30, Wed 9.30–9, Sat 9.30–8 Hôtel de Ville

DEHILLERIN
Full of copper pans, knives, bains-marie, sieves and more. Mail-order service.
H4 18–20 rue Coquillière, 75001 01 42 36 53 13 Mon 9–12.30, 2–6, Tue–Sat 9–6 Les Halles, Louvre-Rivoli

LA DROGUERIE
This gem of a store sells everything you'll need to make your own jewellery, knit or customize accessories.
J4 9 rue du Jour, 75001 01 45 08 93 27 Mon 2–6.45, Tue–Sat 10.30–6.45 Les Halles

FASHION HUBS
Most of the big-name designers are on rue du Faubourg Saint-Honoré and avenue Montaigne, but you'll also find women's high fashion on the place des Victoires (home to Kenzo and Victoire), the rue Étienne-Marcel and towards Les Halles. The Marais's offerings run between rue de Sévigné, rue des Rosiers, place des Vosges and side streets. In Saint-Germain, look along and off boulevard Saint-Germain, on rue de Grenelle and up boulevard Raspail.

FORUM DES HALLES
Underground complex on four levels where some 80 ready-to-wear designers have their boutiques.
J5 1–7 rue Pierre-Lescot, 75001 Mon–Sat 10–8 Châtelet-Les Halles

MARCHÉ DE LA RUE MONTORGUEIL
A marble-paved pedestrian street with trendy bars and lunch places.
J4 Rue Montorgueil, 75001 Food shops Tue–Sat 9–1, 4–7, Sun 9–1 Les Halles

MARIAGE FRÈRES
This tea house, founded in 1854, offers hundreds of teas from all over the world, including some exclusive house blends.
K6 30 rue du Bourg-Tibourg, 75004 01 42 72 28 11 Daily 10.30–7.30; tea room 12–7 Hôtel de Ville

OLIVIERS & CO
Dedicated to olive oil and related products—olive-oil infused biscuits, tapenade and olive-wood bowls.
L6 47 rue Vieille-du-Temple, 75004 01 42 74 38 40 Daily 11–8 Hôtel de Ville

VANESSA BRUNO
This designer's practical, easy-to-wear women's clothing with flair has won her a loyal following.
L5 100 rue Vieille-du-Temple, 75003 01 42 77 19 41 Mon 12.30–7.30, Tue–Sat 10.30–7.30, Sun 2–7 Filles du Calvaire

Entertainment and Nightlife

CAFÉ DE LA DANSE

www.cafedeladanse.com

Pop, rock and world music in an auditorium that feels homey, despite seating more than 300. Also some theatre and dance.

Off map 5 passage Louis-Philipe, 75011 01 47 00 57 59 Bastille

CAFÉ DE L'INDUSTRIE

Friendly, laid-back ambience and flea market decor in this café, a popular meeting place where you can have a drink or an inexpensive bite to eat.

M6 16 rue Saint-Sabin, 75011 01 47 00 13 53 Daily 10am–2am Bréguet-Sabin

DUC DES LOMBARDS

www.ducdeslombards.com

Prestigious jazz musicians regularly play in this Les Halles club.

J5 42 rue des Lombards, 75001 01 42 33 22 88 Closed Sun Châtelet

FORUM DES IMAGES

www.forumdesimages.fr

Films or documentaries shot in or connected with Paris, and film classics. A cheap day pass admits you to four different films. See website for films in other venues.

J5 2 rue du Cinéma, Port Saint-Eustache, Forum des Halles, 75001 01 44 76 63 00 Tue–Fri 12.30–11.30, Sat, Sun 2–11.30 Les Halles, Châtelet

LE FUMOIR

This café and bar, decorated like a gentleman's library in a stately home, offers top-notch cocktails (one of the few places in town to get a real martini) and inventive, tasty food. Always packed, it attracts a stylish, trendy crowd.

H5 6 rue Amiral de Coligny, 75001 01 42 92 00 24 Daily 11am–12.30am Louvre-Rivoli

OPÉRA BASTILLE

www.opera-de-paris.fr

Paris's 'people's' opera house boasts five moveable stages, which make it a technological feat in itself. Performances include opera, operettas, recitals, dance and even theatre.

M7 120 rue de Lyon, 75012 08 92 89 90 90 or 01 40 01 17 89 Bastille

POOLS AND HORSES

Paris's municipal swimming pools have complicated opening hours largely geared to schoolchildren. Phone to check for public hours and avoid Wednesday and Saturday, both popular with children off school. If horse-racing is your passion, don't miss the harness-racing at Vincennes, with its brilliant flashes of colour-coordinated horses and jockeys. Check the racing newspaper *Paris-Turf* for race schedules.

PISCINE DES HALLES (SUZANNE BERLIOUX)

Underground 50m (164ft) pool overlooked by lush tropical garden. The pool has been renovated.

J5 Forum des Halles, 10 place de la Rotonde, 75001 01 42 36 98 44 Les Halles

SUNSET-SUNSIDE

www.sunset-sunside.com

Two jazz clubs: the Sunset offers electric jazz and world music concerts, while the Sunside concentrates on acoustic jazz.

J5 60 rue des Lombards, 75001 01 40 26 46 60 Châtelet

THÉÂTRE DU CHÂTELET

www.chatelet-theatre.com

The Théâtre du Châtelet hosts a varied schedule of opera, symphonic music and dance, as well as popular Sunday morning concerts.

J6 Place du Châtelet, 75001 01 40 28 28 28 Châtelet

THÉÂTRE DE LA VILLE

www.theatredelaville-paris.com

Modern venue with an adventurous agenda of contemporary dance, avant-garde music and plays.

J6 2 place du Châtelet, 75004 01 42 74 22 77 Performances: Mon–Fri 8.30pm, Sat 5pm, 8.30pm Châtelet

Restaurants

PRICES

Prices are approximate, based on a 3-course meal for one person.

€€€	over €90
€€	€30–€90
€	under €30

404 (€€)

This fashionable Moroccan restaurant offers excellent North African cuisine.
K4 69 rue des Gravilliers, 75003 01 42 74 57 81 Daily lunch, dinner Arts et Métiers

AU PIED DU COCHON (€€)

Pigs' trotters feature at this Parisian institution, but there are other delicious offerings, such as seafood and sublime French onion soup, served in elegant surroundings.
J4 6 rue Coquillère, 75001 01 40 13 77 00 Daily 24 hours Les Halles

BENOIT (€€€)

Long-standing Michelin-starred bistro serving classic regional dishes, owned by chef Alain Ducasse. Reserve ahead.
J6 20 rue Saint-Martin, 75004 01 42 72 25 76 Daily lunch, dinner Hôtel de Ville, Châtelet-Les Halles

BISTROT L'OULETTE (€€)

Tiny bistro whose menu homes in on Gascony, cassoulet and duck.
M6 38 rue des Tournelles, 75004 01 42 71 43 33 Mon–Fri lunch, dinner, Sat dinner Bastille

BOFINGER (€€)

Claims to be the oldest brasserie in Paris (1864). Soaring glass dome, lots of mirrors and chandeliers. Seafood, choucroute and steaks.
M6 5 rue de la Bastille, 75004 01 42 72 87 82 Daily lunch, dinner Bastille

CAFÉ DES MUSÉES (€–€€)

Don't let the dull decor fool you: The reasonably priced food is excellent, fresh from the market.
L6 49 rue de Turenne, 75003 01 42 72 96 17 Daily lunch, dinner Saint-Paul, Chemin Vert

GEORGES (€€)

On the top floor of the Pompidou Centre, the inventive modern cuisine is complemented by a stunning view over Paris.
K5 Place Georges-Pompidou, 75004 01 44 78 47 99 Wed–Mon lunch, dinner Rambuteau

CULINARY CONNECTIONS

It is said that Cathérine de Médicis, the Italian wife of Henri II, invented French cuisine in the 16th century—though Gallic opinions may differ. Italian food is very popular in Paris and, in addition to the pizza-and-pasta establishments, there are many fine restaurants specializing in the most sophisticated Italian cuisine.

MONJUL (€€)

Talented chef Julien Agobert produces dishes that are a work of art, and taste as good as they look.
M6 28 rue des Blancs Manteaux, 75004 01 42 74 40 15 Tue–Sat lunch, dinner Rambuteau

LA MUSE VIN (€€)

A bistro and wine bar specializing in natural wines at low prices, with delicious, fresh food in generous helpings.
Off map 101 rue Charonne, 75011 01 40 09 93 05 Mon–Sat dinner only Charonne

PRAMIL (€€)

You can't go wrong with the refined, creative food and reasonable prices in this small, chic restaurant.
L4 9 rue du Vertbois 01 42 72 03 60 Tue–Sat lunch, dinner, Sun dinner Arts et Métiers, Temple

LA TÊTE AILLEURS (€€)

Spacious yet warm Mediterranean-inspired place with chandeliers, stone walls, wall hangings and comfy seating.
L7 20 rue Beautreillis, 75004 01 42 72 47 80 Tue–Fri lunch, dinner, Mon, Sat dinner Saint-Paul, Bastille

Louvre/Champs-Élysées

The world's greatest museum and shopping avenue are conveniently aligned, along with the Arc de Triomphe and the Grande Arche, in La Défense. Make sure your shoes are comfortable before you start exploring.

Parc de Monceau
Monceau
Courcelles
Ternes
Musée Cernuschi
Musée Nissim de Camondo
Arc de Triomphe
Charles de Gaulle-Étoile (+RER)
Musée Jacquemart André
SAINT-HONORÉ
Miromesnil
Saint-Philippe du Roule
Rue du Faubourg Saint-Honoré
George V
Franklin D. Roosevelt
Palais de l'Élysée
Champs-Élysées-Clemenceau
Palais de la Découverte
Grand Palais
Petit Palais
Seine
PONT DES INVALIDES
PONT ALEXANDRE III
COURS LA REINE
AVENUE DES CHAMPS-ÉLYSÉES
BOULEVARD HAUSSMANN
AVENUE GEORGE V
AVENUE FRANKLIN D ROOSEVELT
AVENUE DE WAGRAM
AVENUE MAC-MAHON
AVENUE KLÉBER
AVENUE D'IÉNA
1
2
3
4
5
6
7
0 250 m
0 250 yds
B
C
D
E

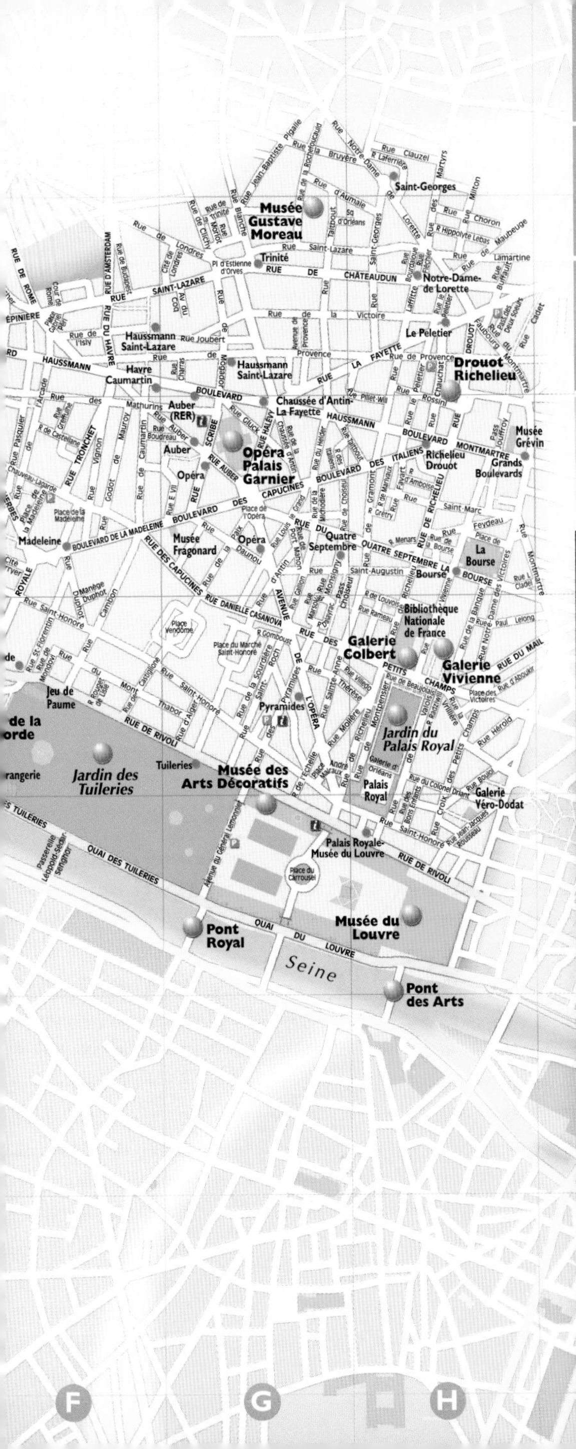

Louvre/Champs-Élysées

Musée Gustave Moreau
Saint-Georges
Trinité
Notre-Dame-de Lorette
Le Peletier
Haussmann Saint-Lazare
Havre Caumartin
Drouot Richelieu
Chaussée d'Antin-La Fayette
Auber (RER)
Auber
Opéra Palais Garnier
Opéra
Musée Grévin
Richelieu Drouot
Grands Boulevards
Madeleine
Musée Fragonard
Quatre Septembre
La Bourse
Bourse
Bibliothèque Nationale de France
Galerie Colbert
Galerie Vivienne
Jeu de Paume
Pyramides
Jardin du Palais Royal
Palais Royal
Jardin des Tuileries
Tuileries
Musée des Arts Décoratifs
Galerie Véro-Dodat
Palais Royale-Musée du Louvre
Musée du Louvre
Pont Royal
Seine
Pont des Arts

RUE SAINT-LAZARE
RUE DE CHÂTEAUDUN
BOULEVARD HAUSSMANN
RUE LA FAYETTE
BOULEVARD DES CAPUCINES
BOULEVARD DES ITALIENS
BOULEVARD MONTMARTRE
RUE DU QUATRE SEPTEMBRE
AVENUE DE L'OPÉRA
RUE DE RIVOLI
QUAI DES TUILERIES
QUAI DU LOUVRE

F
G
H

Arc de Triomphe

The Arc de Triomphe by day (left) and night (right); a detail (middle) of the facade

THE BASICS

www.arc-de-triomphe.monuments-nationaux.fr
B2
Place Charles-de-Gaulle, 75008
01 55 37 73 77
Apr–end Sep daily 10am–11pm; Oct–end Mar daily 10am–10.30pm
Charles de Gaulle-Étoile
Moderate

HIGHLIGHTS

- Views from the terrace
- Liberty
- *La Marseillaise* by François Rude
- Tomb of the Unknown Soldier

TIP

- The museum has touch-sensitive screens illustrating major historical events and the construction of the Arc. Also, a 'real time' film is projected onto the floor, giving the impression of flying 31m (102ft) above the forecourt.

At the hub of Haussmann's web of 12 avenues, which reach out like tentacles towards the city beyond, this is the ultimate symbol of Napoleon's military pretensions and might. Climb the 284 steps to the terrace for superb views.

National symbol Napoleon conceived the Arc de Triomphe as a symbol of his military might in 1806 but it was finished only in 1836 by Louis-Philippe. Two centuries on, the colossal monument is still an image of national pride. It plays a central role in many of France's key commemorations, including VE Day (8 May), Bastille Day (14 July) and Remembrance Day (11 November). Within its grounds are the Tomb of the Unknown Soldier, installed in 1921 after World War I, and a poignant Memorial Flame, added three years later.

Special interest There are wonderful views from the rooftop, 50m (164ft) high. From here you can admire Haussmann's weblike street design and look along the Grand Axis towards place de la Concorde in one direction and the Grande Arche in the other. There is a small shop and recently renovated museum on the way up. At ground level, save time to admire the magnificent sculpted facade, the work of three artists. Don't miss the winged figure of Liberty on François Rude's sculpture *La Marseillaise*, calling the French to defend their nation (northeastern pillar, facing the Champs-Élysées). The 30 shields studding the crown of the arch each bear the name of a Revolutionary or Imperial victory.

The elegant Galerie Vivienne (left and right)

TOP 25

Galeries Vivienne and Colbert

These connecting 19th-century passages, with their original mosaic floors and neoclassical decoration, are a perfect place for people-watching, offering a complete contrast to the trendy buzz of the streets close by.

Shopping arcades Between the late 18th and early 19th centuries the Right Bank included a network of 140 covered passageways—the fashionable shopping malls of the time. Today there are fewer than 30, of which the Galeries Vivienne and Colbert are perhaps the best known, squeezed in between the Bibliothèque Nationale and the place des Victoires. Bookworms and fashion-victims cross paths in this elegant, skylit setting lined with potted palms. It is perfect for a rainy-day browse.

Hive of interest The Galerie Vivienne (1826) opens onto three different streets, while the parallel Galerie Colbert (1826) has its own entrances. Colbert is now completely occupied by the Institut National de l'Histoire de l'Art, but can still be visited, and related exhibitions are held in its gallery. Elegant Galerie Vivienne is commercial in spirit: This is where you can track down designer clothes (Jean Paul Gaultier was one of the first to open a shop here), antiquarian or rare artists' books (a bookshop opened in 1826 at Nos. 45, 46 and 47), contemporary design, fine wines and intriguing toys, or just sit sipping tea beneath the skylight, watching the world go by.

THE BASICS

www.galerie-vivienne.com
H4
Galerie Vivienne: 4 rue des Petits-Champs/6 rue Vivienne, 75002.
Galerie Colbert: 6 rue des Petits-Champs, 75002
Gate at 5 rue de la Banque is open 8–8
Bourse, Palais-Royal, Pyramides
29
Good
Free

HIGHLIGHTS

- Mosaic floor
- Bronze statue
- Staircase at 13 Galerie Vivienne
- Clock
- Chandeliers
- Bookshop

Musée du Louvre

TOP 25

HIGHLIGHTS

- Palace of Khorsabad
- Glass pyramid entrance, designed by I. M. Pei
- *Bataille de San Romano*, Uccello
- *Mona Lisa*, da Vinci
- *La Dentellière*, Vermeer
- *Vénus de Milo*
- Cour Carrée at night
- The Marly Horses

TIP

- To avoid the crowds, visit early morning or Wednesday or Friday evening. Sunday is the busiest day.

Nocturnal lighting transforms the Louvre's glass pyramid entrance into a gigantic cut diamond—just a foretaste of the treasures contained within.

The world's largest museum Since 1981 the Louvre has undergone a radical transformation that crowns six centuries of eventful existence. As a fitting culmination of the project, the museum's star attraction, the *Mona Lisa*, was moved to a room specially refurbished to make viewing the painting easier. Originally a medieval fortress, the Louvre first took shape as a private art gallery under François I, eager to display his Italian loot. Henri IV added several galleries, completed in 1608. After escaping the excesses of the Revolutionary mob, in 1793 it became a people's museum and was later enlarged by Napoleon I, who enriched its collection.

Clockwise from far left: The inverted pyramid inside the Louvre; sculptures in the Richelieu Wing; time to study one of the many paintings in the Louvre; the courtyard; a gallery below ground

Art fortress The vast collection of some 35,000 exhibits is arranged on four floors of three wings: Sully (east), Richelieu (north) and Denon (south), while beneath the elegant Cour Carrée lie the keep and dungeons of the original medieval fortress. The Islamic Arts department now has a new gallery in the Cour Visconti. Almost 5,000 years of art are covered at the museum, starting with Egyptian antiquities and culminating with European painting up to 1848.

Making the most of your visit There is no way that you'll be able to see all 35,000 works on display in one visit, so you'll need to be selective. If you don't know where to start, consider taking one of the *Visite-Découverte* guided tours. The free museum map, available from the information desk, also highlights the key works.

THE BASICS

www.louvre.fr
H5
99 rue de Rivoli, 75001. Main entrance via the pyramid
01 40 20 53 17; Auditorium 01 40 20 55 55
Wed–Mon 9–6 (until 10pm Wed, Fri)
Restaurants and cafés
Palais-Royal–Musée du Louvre
21, 27, 39, 48, 68, 69, 72, 74, 75, 76, 81, 85, 95
Excellent
Moderate until 6pm; inexpensive after 6pm on late nights and Sun; free first Sun of every month
Tours, audioguides, lectures, films, workshops, concerts. Buy your ticket online to save a long wait

Opéra Palais Garnier

A detail (left) of the exterior of the Opéra Palais Garnier (right and opposite)

THE BASICS

www.operadeparis.fr
G3
Place de l'Opéra, 75009
Information, reservations 0892 89 90 90 (34¢ per min)
Daily 10–4.30
Bar open during shows
Opéra
20, 21, 22, 27, 29, 42, 52, 53, 66, 68, 81, 95
RER Line A, Auber
Few; call for appointment, tel 01 40 01 18 50
Moderate
Guided tours (1.5 hours) in English on Wed, Sat, Sun 11.30, 2.30; daily 11.30, 2.30 Jul, Aug (expensive, tel 0825 05 44 05)

HIGHLIGHTS

- Grand Staircase
- Grand Foyer
- Auditorium
- Facade
- Lamp-bearers
- The new shop, Galerie de l'Opéra de Paris (▷ 84)

This is an ornate wedding cake of a building, but the sumptuous and riotous details that decorate its every surface are in fact the perfect epitaph to the frenetic architectural activities of France's Second Empire.

Past glory When Charles Garnier's opera house was inaugurated in 1875 it marked the end of Haussmann's ambitious urban facelift and announced the sociocultural movement to the Belle Époque, with Nijinksy and Diaghilev's Ballets Russes as later highlights. Today the Salle Garnier stages both dance and opera. Rudolf Nureyev was director of the Paris Ballet here between 1983 and 1989.

Dazzle Competing with a series of provocative lamp-bearing statues, the Palais Garnier's extravagant, regilded facade of arches, winged horses, friezes and columns is topped by a verdigris dome and leads into a majestic foyer. This is dominated by the Grand Staircase, dripping with balconies and chandeliers, in turn sweeping upwards to the Grand Foyer and its gilded mirrors, marble, murals and Murano glass. Do not miss the equally ornate auditorium, with its dazzling gold-leaf decorations and red-velvet seats, and Marc Chagall's incongruous ceiling. The auditorium can be visited except during rehearsals. The opera house also has a library and a museum of operatic memorabilia. The building's renovation has removed the layer of black soot that used to cover it, leaving it simply resplendent.

ACADEMIE NATIONALE DE MUSIQUE

Place de la Concorde

The place de la Concorde by day (left) and floodlit at night (right)

THE BASICS

- E4–F4
- Place de la Concorde, 75008
- Jeu de Paume 01 47 03 12 50; www.jeudepaume.org; Musée de l'Orangerie 01 44 77 80 07; www.musee-orangerie.fr
- Jeu de Paume Tue 12–9, Wed–Fri 12–7, Sat, Sun 10–7; Musée de l'Orangerie Wed–Mon 9–6
- Concorde
- 24, 42, 52, 72, 73, 84, 94
- Jeu de Paume/Musée de l'Orangerie moderate
- Jeu de Paume annexe in Hôtel de Sully, 62 rue Saint-Antoine Saint-Paul

HIGHLIGHTS

- Jeu de Paume
- Musée de l'Orangerie
- Hôtel de Crillon (▷ 112)
- *Chevaux de Marly* (reproductions)
- View up the Champs-Élysées

As you stand in this noisy, traffic-choked square it is hard to imagine the crowds baying for the deaths of Louis XVI and Marie-Antoinette, who were both guillotined here at the height of the French Revolution.

Chop-chop This pulsating square was initially laid out in the mid-18th century to accommodate a statue of King Louis XV. Under the new name of place de la Révolution, it then witnessed the mass executions of the French Revolution and was finally renamed the place de la Concorde in 1795, as revolutionary zeal abated. In the same year Guillaume Coustou's *Chevaux de Marly* were erected at the base of the Champs-Élysées (today reproductions; the originals are in the Louvre). Crowning the middle of the Concorde is a 3,000-year-old Egyptian obelisk overlooking eight symbolic statues of French cities. Use the pedestrian crossing to reach the central island for a closer look at the obelisk, framed by two fountains.

Grandeur To the north, on either side of the rue Royale, stand the colonnaded Hôtel de Crillon (on the left) and the matching Hôtel de la Marine (right), pre-Revolutionary relics. The rue Royale, with its luxury establishments, leads to the Madeleine. The eastern side of the Concorde is dominated by two public art galleries, both in the Jardin des Tuileries (▷ 81). The Jeu de Paume focuses on photography. The beautifully renovated Orangerie (nearer the river) is famous for its panels of Monet's *Water Lilies* and its Impressionist paintings.

More to See

DROUOT RICHELIEU

www.drouot.fr

Paris's main auction rooms, where a Persian carpet or a Louis XV commode may come under the hammer.

H2 9 rue Drouot, 75009 01 48 00 20 20 Mon–Sat 11–6 (most auctions start at 2pm); closed Aug Richelieu-Drouot

JARDIN DU PALAIS ROYAL

Elegant 18th-century arcades surround this peaceful garden and palace (now the Conseil Constitutionnel and the Ministère de la Culture). Daniel Buren's conceptual striped columns occupy the Cour d'Honneur.

H4 Place du Palais-Royal, 75001 Apr, May daily 7am–10.15pm; Jun–end Aug daily 7am–11pm; Sep daily 7am–9.30pm; Oct–end Mar daily 7.30am–8.30pm Plenty Palais-Royal–Musée du Louvre

JARDIN DES TUILERIES

This park offers superb views of the Louvre and Eiffel Tower, as well as two art galleries (▷ 80), outdoor cafés and two large ponds (children can rent model yachts to sail on the one nearest the Louvre). Laid out in 1564 and later formalized by Le Nôtre, it is now replanted to match the Louvre.

F4–5/G4–5 Place de la Concorde, 75001 Apr–end Jun, Sep daily 7.30am–9pm; Jul, Aug daily 7.30am–11.45pm (closes one hour later Sat, Sun); Oct–end Mar 7.30–7.30 Cafés Tuileries Free

MUSÉE DES ARTS DÉCORATIFS

www.lesartsdecoratifs.fr

A magnificent collection of decorative arts in a beautifully restored space. Throughout the 20th century contributions by designers such as Le Corbusier, Mallet-Stevens, Nikki de Saint Phalle and Philippe Starck greatly enriched the collections.

G5 107 rue de Rivoli, 75001 01 44 55 57 50 Tue–Fri 11–6 (until 9 Thu), Sat, Sun 10–6 Palais-Royal–Musée du Louvre Moderate

MUSÉE GUSTAVE MOREAU

www.musee-moreau.fr

This studio-museum, on the edge of Pigalle, offers an intriguing view of

Columns by Daniel Buren, in the courtyard of the Palais Royal

how a late-19th-century artist lived. On the lower floors are the studios of the Symbolist painter Gustave Moreau (1826–98), teacher to Henri Matisse. Upstairs is a reconstruction of his private apartment. Paintings gracing his walls include works by Edgar Degas and Théodore Chassériau.
G2 14 rue de la Rochefoucauld, 75009 01 48 74 38 50 Wed–Mon 10–12.45, 2–5.15 Moderate; free to all on first Sun of month Trinité

MUSÉE JACQUEMART-ANDRÉ

www.musee-jacquemart-andre.com
An elegant mansion hosts this fine collection of around 150 paintings, including works by Botticelli, Rembrandt, Bellini and Van Dyck.
D2 158 boulevard Haussmann, 75008 01 45 62 11 59 Daily 10–6 Saint-Philippe-du-Roule, Miromesnil Moderate (audioguide included)

PARC DE MONCEAU

This classic park, redesigned in 1793 by Thomas Blaikie, is full of follies and picturesque faux ruins.
D1 35 boulevard de Courcelles, 75008 Apr–end Oct daily 7am–10pm; Nov–end Mar 7am–8pm Monceau Free

PONT DES ARTS

The pedestrian bridge of 1804 was replaced in 1984 by a new iron structure of seven steel arches crossed by resonant wooden planks. It's a popular spot for impromptu parties and street performances.
H5–6 Louvre-Rivoli

PONT ROYAL

Five classical arches join the Tuileries with the Faubourg Saint-Germain area. Built in 1689 by Gabriel to Mansart's design, it was once used for major Parisian festivities and fireworks.
G5 Palais-Royal–Musée du Louvre

RUE DU FAUBOURG SAINT-HONORÉ

Price tags and politics cohabit in this street of luxury. See Hermès' imaginative window dressing or salute the gendarmes in front of the Élysée Palace.
E3 Madeleine, Miromesnil

Enjoying a spring day in the Parc de Monceau

Pont des Arts crosses the Seine

Rive Droite Walk

This walk takes in two stately gardens and numerous historical monuments in the heart of Paris.

DISTANCE: 3.5km (2 miles) **ALLOW:** 1 hour 30 minutes

START

PLACE DE LA CONCORDE (▷ 80)
Concorde, bus 24, 42, 72, 73, 84, 94

❶ Carefully cross the stream of traffic flowing through place de la Concorde to take a look at the obelisk in the heart of this historic square.

❷ Cross to the ornate gates of the Jardin des Tuileries (▷ 81) and stroll through this vibrant public garden. At the end of the park, turn left to reach rue de Rivoli.

❸ Turn right onto rue de Rivoli and walk alongside the Louvre (▷ 76–77). Cross rue de Rivoli into place du Palais-Royal. From here, cross rue Saint-Honoré and bear left.

❹ Between the Comédie Française and the palace, enter the Jardin du Palais Royal (▷ 81) through an arch left of the palace. Walk the length of the garden to rue de Beaujolais.

❺ Take rue Vivienne for a short distance, then go left onto rue des Petits Champs.

❻ You'll pass the Bibliothèque Nationale de France as you walk along this road. Continue until you reach avenue de l'Opéra.

❼ Cross the avenue and walk to the right towards the opera house (▷ 78). Just before place de l'Opéra, turn left down rue de la Paix, with elegant jewellery shops. This leads to the even more exclusive place Vendôme.

❽ Cross the square, walk down rue de Castiglione, with its arcades. Turn right onto rue de Rivoli to return to place de la Concorde.

END

PLACE DE LA CONCORDE
Concorde, bus 24, 42, 72, 73, 84, 94

Shopping

À LA MÈRE DE FAMILLE

Original 18th-century grocery shop with shelves laden with imaginatively created chocolates, jams and unusual groceries.
H2 33–35 rue du Faubourg Montmartre, 75009 01 47 70 83 69 Tue–Sat 8.15–1.30, 3–7 Le Peletier, Cadet

CHALCOGRAPHIE DU LOUVRE

Take home something unusual: a real engraving hand-printed from one of the Louvre's collection of 13,000 artist's plates.
G5 Carrousel du Louvre, 75001 01 40 20 59 35 Thu–Sun 9.30–7, Mon, Wed 9.30–9.30 Palais Royal

CHANEL

Classy yet sexy, Chanel's fashion embodies Parisian elegance.
F3 31 rue Cambon, 75001 01 42 86 28 00 Mon–Sat 10–7 Madeleine, Concorde

COLETTE

The place to go for leading design in fashion and home furnishings. The water bar serves more than 100 brands.
G4 213 rue Saint-Honoré, 75001 01 55 35 33 90 Mon–Sat 11–7 Tuileries, Pyramides

DIDIER LUDOT

Rare vintage designer clothes (Chanel, Dior, Balmain) and classic Hermès handbags. Picturesque location.
H4 20–24 Galerie Montpensier, 75001 01 42 96 06 56 Mon–Sat 10.30–7 Palais-Royal–Musée du Louvre

GALERIE DE L'OPÉRA DE PARIS

This new boutique-bookshop focuses on opera and choreography, with all the latest CDs and books, as well as postcards, posters and presents.
G3 Opéra Palais Garnier, rue Halévy, 75009 No phone Mon–Sat 10–6.30, Sun 10–5 Opéra

DEPARTMENT STORES

Printemps and Galeries Lafayette, in the prestigious boulevard Haussmann, each stock hundreds of brands—from fashion to designer homeware. Printemps (Mon–Wed, Fri, Sat 9.35–7, Thu 9.35am–10pm Havre-Caumartin) claims to have Europe's largest beauty department. Don't miss the art nouveau stained-glass cupola on the sixth floor of Printemps de la Mode, or the view from the ninth floor of Printemps de la Maison. At Galeries Lafayette (Mon–Wed, Fri, Sat 9.30–7.30, Thu 9.30–9 Chaussée d'Antin) highlights include the 1912 Byzantine-style glass dome and the Lafayette Gourmet food hall.

IKI MEZURA

Beautiful shoes that are constantly re-invented to change with the seasons. The workmanship and finish are impeccable.
G4 318 rue Saint-Honoré, 75001 01 40 20 47 37 Tue–Sat 10.30–7, Sun, Mon 2.30–7 Saint-Paul

LOUIS VUITTON

The ultimate brand name's store on the Champs-Élysées, conceived as a continuation of a promenade on the avenue, has people lining up to get inside.
C3 101 avenue des Champs-Élysées, 75008 0810 810 010 Mon–Sat 10–8, Sun 11–7 George V

LOUVRE DES ANTIQUAIRES

www.louvre-antiquaires.com
Huge, modernized complex of antiques shops. You'll find everything from Eastern carpets to furniture, silver, porcelain and paintings. Good quality but expect high prices.
H5 2 place du Palais-Royal, 75001 01 42 97 27 27 Tue–Sun 11–7 (closed Sun in Jul and Aug) Palais-Royal–Musée du Louvre

SI TU VEUX

Charming toy shop with affordable and interesting toys, games and dressing-up gear. Separate section devoted to teddy bears.
H4 68 Galerie Vivienne, 75002 01 42 60 59 97 Tue–Sat 10–7 Bourse

Entertainment and Nightlife

AUDITORIUM DU LOUVRE

www.louvre.fr

A high-quality and varied series of lunchtime and evening concerts in an impressive 450-seat auditorium beneath the Louvre's pyramid.

G5 Musée du Louvre (entrance by the pyramid), 75001 01 40 20 55 55 Palais-Royal

LE BALZAC

www.cinemabalzac.com

Le Balzac is famous for its screenings of American independent films (in the original language) and for the debates that often follow. The biggest of the three screens often has photography exhibitions and concerts are held before Saturday evening screenings. Bar on site.

B3 1 rue Balzac, 75008 01 45 61 10 60 George V, Charles de Gaulle–Étoile

LE BARON

Once a high-class hostess club and now a hot nightspot that attracts stars and VIPs, Le Baron was founded by trendy graffiti artist André and features top DJs.

B4 6 avenue Marceau, 75008 01 47 20 04 01 Alma-Marceau, Étoile

BARRAMUNDI

www.barramundi.fr

Draws a fashionable crowd with its world music, bar, lounge and French restaurant.

H3 3 rue Taitbout, 75009 01 47 70 21 21 Mon–Fri 12–3pm, 6.30pm–2am, Sat 7pm–2am Richelieu-Drouot, Chaussée d'Antin

LA BELLE ÉPOQUE

www.belleepoqueparis.com

The truly sparkling show La Vie est Belle (Life is Beautiful) includes the cancan, which the audience is then invited to dance. Fine French cuisine is served during the show.

G4 36 rue des Petits-Champs, 75002 01 42 96 33 33 Show: daily 9pm Pyramides

CLUB L'ARC

www.larc-paris.com

Formerly called L'Étoile, this restaurant/club opposite the Arc de Triomphe is ideal for sipping cocktails from the huge, covered terrace. The ambience is chic, vintage and intimate.

B3 12 rue de Presbourg, 75016 01 45 00 78 70 Restaurant Mon–Fri lunch, dinner, Sat dinner. Club Fri, Sat midnight–6am Charles de Gaulle–Étoile

BEAUTIFUL PEOPLE

The clubs around the Champs-Élysées tend to attract VIPs, celebrities and a generally well-heeled crowd. Nightclubs usually don't open until 11pm or midnight, with the dancing continuing until dawn. For a younger, more laid-back, arty bar scene, go to the bar-lined rue Oberkampf or the Canal Saint-Martin area. The Marais district is also packed with bars.

COMÉDIE FRANÇAISE/ SALLE RICHELIEU

www.comedie-francaise.fr

The Comédie Française, home to France's most prestigious troupe of actors, was founded by Louis XIV in 1680. Today, the repertoire is made up of the classics, including works by Shakespeare, Molière, and a few modern pieces.

G5 1 place Colette, 75001 08 25 10 16 80 Performance daily 8.30pm, some matinées Sat, Sun Palais-Royal–Musée du Louvre

HARRY'S NEW YORK BAR

www.harrys-bar.fr

Popular with the British and French, this bar offers hundreds of cocktails.

G3 5 rue Daunou, 75002 01 42 61 71 14 Mon–Sat 11am–4am, Sun noon–3am Opéra

QUEEN

www.queen.fr

This large club is still going strong and is popular with both straights and gays. Top DJs, with different themes each evening.

C3 102 avenue des Champs-Élysées, 75008 0892 70 73 30 Daily midnight–7am George V

Restaurants

Prices are approximate, based on a 3-course meal for one person.
€€€ over €90
€€ €30–€90
€ under €30

6 NEW YORK (€€)

6 New York offers beautiful contemporary decor and fusion food.
B4 6 avenue de New York, 75016 01 40 70 03 30 Mon–Fri lunch, dinner, Sat dinner Alma-Marceau

BISTRO ROMAIN (€–€€)

The decor is reminiscent of an Italian opera house, while the menu is not so refined, but you'll find excellent value pasta as well as divine chocolate mousse. There are 18 Bistro Romains in the city.
D3 26 avenue des Champs-Élysées, 75008 01 53 75 17 84 Daily 11.30am–1am Franklin D. Roosevelt

CAFÉ MARLY (€€)

This classy café-restaurant in the Louvre itself must have the best terrace in the world, with its view of I. M. Pei's glass pyramid and the opposite wing of the museum behind it. The food is reliably good, the service friendly and the interior elegant.
G5 93 rue de Rivoli, 75001 01 49 26 06 60 Daily 7am–2am Palais-Royal–Musée du Louvre

CARRÉ DES FEUILLANTS (€€€)

Elegant setting for Alain Dutournier's brilliant evocation of the cooking of his native Gascony. He uses the best ingredients to wonderful effect, earning two Michelin stars.
F4 14 rue de Castiglione, 75001 01 42 86 82 82 Mon–Fri lunch, dinner. Closed Aug Tuileries

LE CÉLADON (€€€)

Interesting variations on French classics, including bass with ginger vinegar and roast figs with pepper ice cream.
G3 Hotel Westminster, 15 rue Daunou, 75002 01 47 03 40 42 Mon–Fri lunch, dinner. Closed Aug Opéra

GUY SAVOY (€€€)

A gastronomic temple, where Guy Savoy makes cooking an art form. The restaurant has three Michelin stars.
B2 18 rue Troyon, 75017 01 43 80 40 61 Tue–Fri lunch, dinner, Sat dinner Charles de Gaulle–Étoile

NEW BISTROS

Paris may be the food capital of the world, with more than its share of top restaurants, but not everyone can afford the astronomical prices of the best eateries. About 10 years ago a few famous chefs opened 'baby bistros', which benefited from their expertise but offered fine meals in often nondescript surroundings for reasonable prices. The trend has now expanded and Paris is full of 'nouveaux bistros'.

LE SENDERENS (€€€)

Tired of all the fuss of owning a Michelin three-star restaurant, Alain Senderens closed down Lucas Carton and opened the simpler and somewhat less expensive Le Senderens. Michelin wasn't intimidated, however, and awarded the restaurant two stars.
F3 9 place de la Madeleine, 75008 01 42 65 22 90 Daily lunch, dinner (closed 2–24 Aug) Madeleine

SPOON (€€€)

Trendy bistro-style restaurant with open kitchen. Chef Alain Ducasse's highly original 'world food' menu lets you mix and match.
C4 12 rue de Marignan, 75008 01 40 76 34 44 Mon–Fri lunch, dinner. Closed Aug, 25 Dec–3 Jan Franklin D. Roosevelt

TAILLEVENT (€€€)

Discreetly elegant restaurant. The cooking has classical foundations, with subtle modern leanings. Two Michelin stars.
C2 15 rue Lamennais, 75008 01 44 95 15 01 Mon–Fri lunch, dinner. Closed Aug George V, Charles de Gaulle–Étoile

The cliché is right: Montmartre is a village. Topped by the Sacré-Cœur, it has not changed much since Utrillo painted its steep streets and Picasso whipped out masterpieces in his Bateau Lavoir studio.

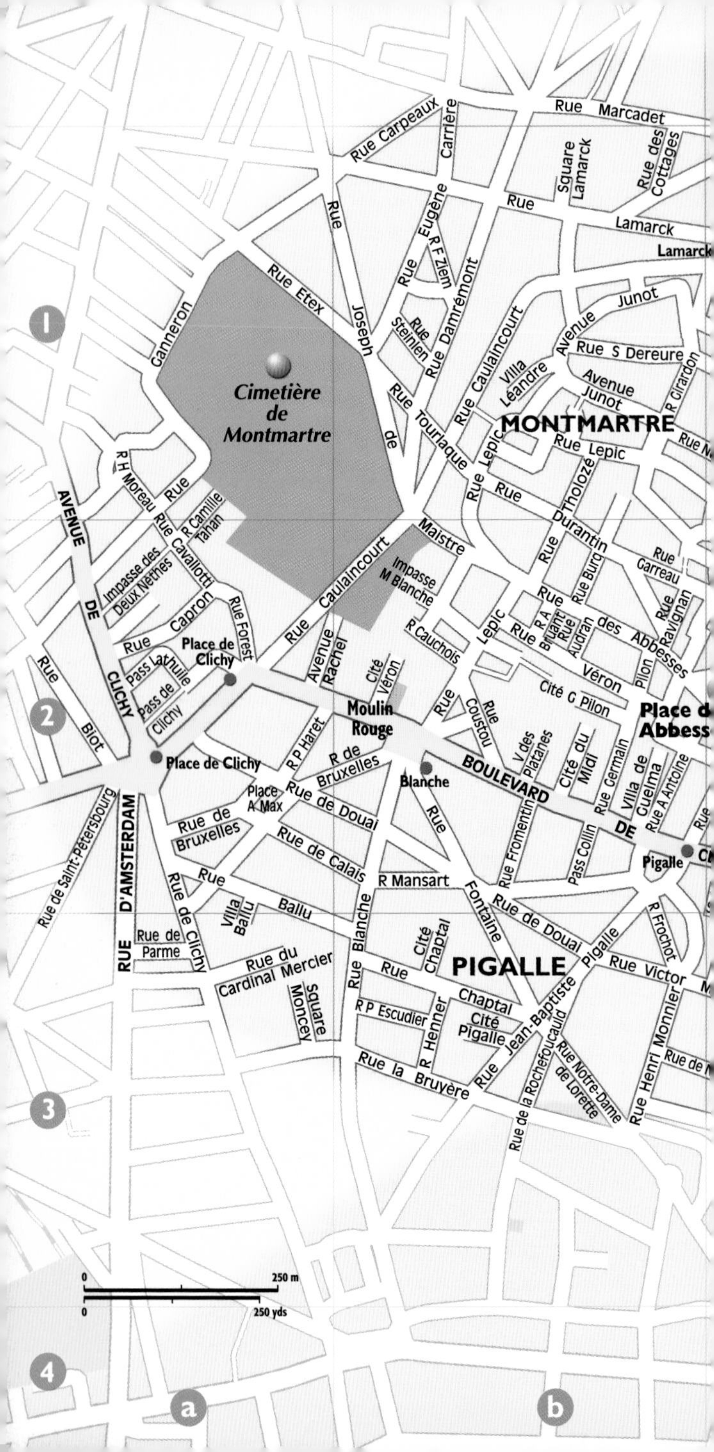

Rue Marcadet
Rue Carpeaux
Carrière
Square Lamarck
Rue des Cottages
Rue Lamarck
Lamarck
Rue Eugène
R F Ziem
Rue Joseph de Maistre
Rue Etex
Rue Damrémont
Rue Steinlen
Ganneron
Cimetière de Montmartre
Avenue Junot
Rue S Dereure
Rue Caulaincourt
Villa Léandre
R Girardon
MONTMARTRE
Rue Tourlaque
Rue Lepic
Rue Tholozé
Rue Durantin
R H Moreau
Rue Cavallotti
R Camille Tahan
AVENUE DE CLICHY
Impasse des Deux Nethes
Rue Capron
Rue Forest
Impasse M Blanche
Rue Burq
Rue Garreau
Rue Ravignan
R A Bruant
Rue Audran
Rue des Abbesses
R Cauchois
Place de Clichy
Pass Lathuile
Pass de Clichy
Avenue Rachel
Cité Véron
Rue Véron
Cité G Pilon
Rue Pilon
Rue Biot
Moulin Rouge
Rue Coustou
V des Platanes
Cité du Midi
Rue Germain
Villa de Guelma
Rue A Antoine
Place des Abbesses
R P Haret
R de Bruxelles
Blanche
BOULEVARD DE CLICHY
Place A Max
Rue de Douai
Rue de Bruxelles
Rue de Saint-Pétersbourg
RUE D'AMSTERDAM
Rue de Calais
Rue Fromentin
Pass Collin
Pigalle
R Mansart
Rue Fontaine
Rue Ballu
Villa Ballu
Rue de Clichy
Rue de Parme
Rue Blanche
Cité Chaptal
Rue Chaptal
PIGALLE
Rue Pigalle
R Frochot
Rue Victor Massé
Rue du Cardinal Mercier
Square Moncey
R P Escudier
R Henner
Cité Pigalle
Rue Jean-Baptiste Pigalle
Rue Henri Monnier
Rue de la Rochefoucauld
Rue Notre-Dame de Lorette
Rue la Bruyère
0
250 m
0
250 yds
1
2
3
4
a
b

Montmartre

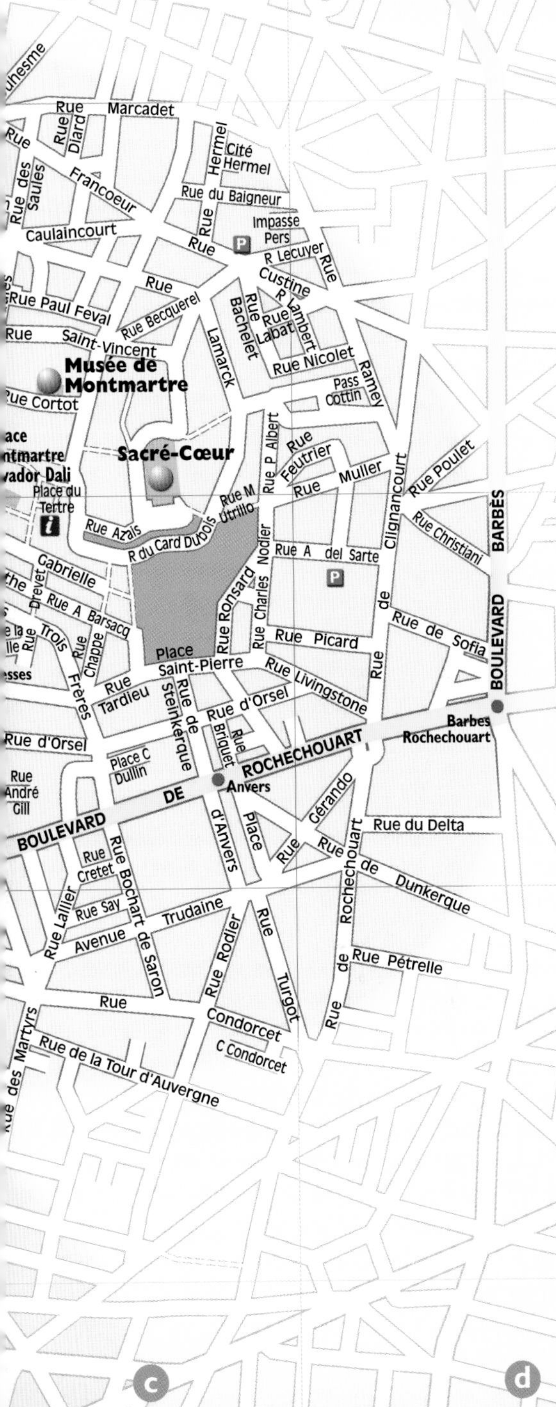

Rue Marcadet
Rue Diard
Rue des Saules
Rue Francoeur
Rue Hermel
Cité Hermel
Rue du Baigneur
Caulaincourt
Rue
Impasse Pers
R Lecuyer
Rue Custine
Rue Paul Feval
Rue Becquerel
Rue Saint-Vincent
Rue Bachelet
Rue Labat
R Lambert
Rue Lamarck
Rue Nicolet
Ramey
Pass Cottin
Musée de Montmartre
Rue Cortot
Sacré-Cœur
Place du Tertre
Rue P Albert
Rue Feutrier
Rue Muller
Rue M Utrillo
Rue Azais
R du Card Dubois
Rue Poulet
Rue Christiani
Rue de Clignancourt
Rue A del Sarte
Rue Charles Nodier
Rue Ronsard
Gabrielle
Drevet
Rue A Barsacq
Rue Chappe
Rue des Trois Frères
Rue Picard
Rue de Sofia
Place Saint-Pierre
Rue Livingstone
Rue Tardieu
Rue de Steinkerque
Rue d'Orsel
Rue Briquet
BOULEVARD BARBÈS
Barbes Rochechouart
BOULEVARD DE ROCHECHOUART
Place C Dullin
Rue André Gill
Anvers
Rue Gérando
Rue du Delta
Place d'Anvers
Rue Cretet
Rue Bochart de Saron
Rue de Dunkerque
Rue de Rochechouart
Rue Say
Avenue Trudaine
Rue Lallier
Rue Rodier
Rue Turgot
Rue Pétrelle
Rue Condorcet
C Condorcet
Rue des Martyrs
Rue de la Tour d'Auvergne
c
d

Sacré-Cœur

TOP 25

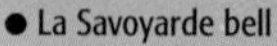

HIGHLIGHTS

- La Savoyarde bell
- View from the dome
- Mosaic of Christ
- Treasure of Sacré-Cœur
- Bronze doors at Saint-Pierre
- Stained-glass gallery
- Statue of Christ
- Statue of Virgin Mary and Child
- The funicular ride from place Saint-Pierre
- Hearing the choir sing during a service

TIP

- Sacré-Cœur is a 10-minute walk from Abbesses or Anvers Métro. Or you could take the Montmartrobus to the base of the funicular.

Few people would admit it, but the high point of a trip up here is not the basilica itself but the stunning views. You can't forget, however, that Sacré-Cœur was built in memory of the 58,000 dead of the Franco-Prussian War.

Weighty Although construction started in 1875, it was not until 1914 that this white neo-Romanesque-Byzantine edifice was completed, partly due to the problems of laying foundations in the quarry-riddled hill of Montmartre. Priests still work in relays to maintain the tradition of perpetual prayer for forgiveness for the horrors of war and atonement for the deaths of 58,000 people during the Franco-Prussian war of 1870–71 and the massacre of some 20,000 Communards by government troops. The square

Clockwise from top left: A view across Paris from the busy steps of Sacré-Cœur; statue of Cardinal Guibert; walking up the steps in front of Sacré-Cœur; the interior lit up at night; a weathered gargoyle on the exterior of the basilica

bell tower was an afterthought and houses one of the world's heaviest bells, La Savoyarde, which weighs in at 19 tons. The stained-glass windows are replacements of those that were shattered by enemy bombs in 1944.

Panoramas This unmistakable feature of the Paris skyline magnetizes the crowds arriving by funicular or via the steep steps of the terraced garden. Dawn and dusk offer sparkling panoramas over the city, especially from the exterior terrace of the dome, the second-highest point in Paris after the Eiffel Tower (access is from the left-hand side of the basilica, in rue du Cardinal Guibert). Just to the west of Sacré-Cœur is the diminutive Saint-Pierre, a much reworked though charming church that is all that remains of the Benedictine abbey of Montmartre founded in 1133.

THE BASICS

www.sacre-coeur-montmartre.fr

c1

Place du Parvis du Sacré-Cœur, 75018

01 53 41 89 09

Daily 6am–10.30pm; dome and crypt 9–5.45

Abbesses (from here, walk along rue Yvonne Le Tac and rue Tardieu, then take funicular or walk up steps) or Anvers

Montmartrobus, 30, 31, 54, 80, 85

Wheelchair access from back of basilica

Basilica and crypt free; dome moderate

More to See

CIMETIÈRE DE MONTMARTRE

Montmartre's cemetery is packed with graves of the famous, including composers Hector Berlioz and Jacques Offenbach, writers Henri Stendhal and Alexandre Dumas, artists Edgar Degas and Jean-Baptiste Greuze, film-maker François Truffaut and singer Dalida. The imposing tomb of Émile Zola is close to the flower-filled roundabout near the main entrance, although the writer's remains were moved to the Panthéon in 1908. A noticeboard at the main entrance gives times and dates of guided visits.

a1 20 avenue Rachel, 75018 01 53 42 36 30 Mid-Mar to end Oct Mon–Fri 8–6, Sat 8.30–6, Sun 9–6; Nov to mid-Mar Mon–Sat 8–5.30, Sun 9–5.30 (last entry 15 mins before closing) Place de Clichy–Blanche

MUSÉE DE MONTMARTRE

www.museedemontmartre.fr

Montmartre's history is arguably the most enchanting of all Paris's districts, with its walking beheaded saint, prosperous windmills and infamous nightlife. You can find out more at the unassuming Musée de Montmartre, in a delightful 17th-century mansion that once belonged to a member of Molière's stage troupe. The house, behind Montmartre's one remaining vineyard, later welcomed the painter Pierre-Auguste Renoir.

c1 12 rue Cortot, 75018 01 49 25 89 37 Tue–Sun 11–6 (until 7 Fri–Sun in Aug) Lamarck Caulaincourt, Anvers

PLACE DES ABBESSES

Place des Abbesses is less touristy than place du Tertre, farther up the Montmartre hill, so it's a quieter coffee stop. The magnificent art nouveau Métro entrance here leads into Paris's deepest station, 30m (98.5ft) below ground. The church of Saint-Jean-de-Montmartre (1904) picks up on the art nouveau theme, with decorative windows that enliven the rather ugly redbrick cladding. The square takes its name from the abbey that once stood on the site.

c2 Place des Abbesses, Montmartre, 75018 Abbesses

Cimitière de Montmartre

Place des Abbesses Métro station

Montmartre Walk

Enjoy a tour of the picturesque little streets behind the scenes of the touristy Sacré-Cœur.

DISTANCE: 3km (2 miles) **ALLOW:** 2 hours

START

PLACE BLANCHE
Blanche 30, 54, 68, 74, 95

❶ Start from place Blanche, walk west along boulevard de Clichy, past the Moulin Rouge (▷ 95). Turn right into avenue Rachel to the entrance of the Cimetière de Montmartre (▷ 92).

❷ Return to avenue Rachel and go up the steps on the right to rue Caulaincourt. Turn right and go to the junction with rue Joseph de Maistre.

❸ Turn right and soon sharp left up rue Lepic. Head to the junction with rue Tholozé. Farther along the road turn left into rue Girardon. Cross avenue Junot.

❹ Enter square Suzanne-Buisson. Facing the statue, turn right and head into place Casadesus, in rue Simon Dereure. Turn right, up the stairs, to the allée des Brouillards.

❺ Continue to place Dalida then walk up the cobbled rue de l'Abreuvoir.

❻ Turn left after La Maison Rose and walk down steep rue des Saules to Au Lapin Agile. Turn right along rue Saint-Vincent, past the vineyard. Cross rue du Mont Cenis, and walk up to rue de la Bonne and into the Parc de la Turlure.

❼ Across the park, exit onto rue du Chevalier de la Barre. Turn right, then left on rue du Cardinal Guibert to Sacré-Cœur (▷ 90–91). Turn right along rue Azaïs and right again up rue Saint-Eleuthère to Saint-Pierre-de-Montmartre.

❽ Turn left, cross place du Tertre to leave by rue Norvins. Second left, go through place Jean-Baptiste Clément. Turn right into rue Ravignan, and continue left into place Émile Goudeau. To leave the square, walk down a small flight of steps and continue down rue Ravignan until you reach rue des Abbesses. Turn left here to place des Abbesses.

END

PLACE DES ABBESSES (▷ 92)
Abbesses Montmartrobus

Shopping

BASE ONE

Clubland meets designer chic in this boutique, housed in what seems to be an elegant sitting room. Owners Princesse Léa and Jean-Louis Faverole are doyens of clubland and have an excellent eye for what's up-and-coming in the fashion scene.

c2 47 bis rue d'Orsel, 75018 01 53 28 04 52 Tue–Sat 12.30–8, Sun 3.30–8 Anvers

BOULANGERIE DELMONTEL

This bakery and pastry shop stands out on a street known for its many mouthwatering food shops. Arnaud Delmontel won the city of Paris's prize for best baguette in 2007 and became official supplier to the presidential residence.

c3 39 rue des Martyrs, 75009 01 48 78 29 33 Mon, Wed–Sat 7am–8.30pm, Sun 7–2.30 Notre-Dame-de-Lorette

CHARCUTERIE LYONNAISE

You will find the specialties of Lyon here, including sublime *jambon persillé* and sausages.

c3 58 rue des Martyrs, 75009 01 48 78 96 45 Mon–Sat 9–9, Sun 9–1 Anvers

DETAILLE

This Paris beauty shop, which recently celebrated its centenary, was opened by the Countess de Presle, one of the first people in Paris to own an automobile and the inventor of the store's best-selling antipollution face cream, Baume Automobile.

H2 10 rue Saint-Lazare, 75009 01 48 78 68 50 Mon 3–7, Tue–Sat 10–1, 2–7 Notre-Dame-de-Lorette

JUDITH LACROIX

High-end, very chic children's clothing. Nice styles for *maman,* too

b3 3 rue Henri Monnier, 75009 01 48 78 22 37 Mon–Sat 10–7 Saint-Georges

KAMILLE

Boutique selling beautifully cut women's clothes in natural fabrics, many designed by the owner.

c2 53 rue d'Orsel, 75018 01 53 28 15 07 Mon–Fri 11–7, Sat 11–5 Abbesses

BOUTIQUING

The streets around the Abbesses Métro station offer a treasure trove of quirky independent clothing, accessories and gift boutiques. For fabulous food shops head down the rue des Abbesses and turn left on rue Lepic. Another wonderful food shopping area in Montmartre is the stretch of rue des Martyrs that descends below the boulevard de Clichy.

LIBRAIRIE DES ABBESSES

A great little bookshop for those who read French or want to practise. Also has beautiful art books.

c2 30 rue Yvonne le Tac, 75018 01 46 06 84 30 Mon 11–8, Tue–Fri 9.30–8, Sat 10–8, Sun 12–8 Abbesses

MARCHÉ BARBÈS

Come to this colourful market for ethnic wares, scarves or fruit and veg.

Off map at d2 Boulevard de la Chapelle, 75018 Wed 7–2.30, Sat 7–3 Barbès-Rochechouart

MARCHÉ DE LA RUE LEPIC

It's up a steep hill but worth the effort to explore this atmospheric street, made famous in the film *Amélie* (2001). The best food shops are from the junction with rue des Abbesses down to boulevard de Clichy.

b2 Rue Lepic and rue des Abbesses, 75018 Most shops open Tue–Sat 9–1, 4–7, Sun 9–1 Abbesses, Blanche

PETIT BATEAU

A chain known for the excellent quality of its children's shirts. Every grown-up Parisienne has a Petit Bateau T-shirt—considered the best-fitting and the starting block for chic.

b2 50 rue des Abbesses, 75018 01 42 52 81 76 Mon–Sat 10–7 Abbesses

Entertainment and Nightlife

BOUFFES DU NORD
www.bouffesdunord.com
Many plays staged by director Peter Brook are not only excellent but also in English.
✚ Off map at d2 ✉ 37 bis boulevard de la Chapelle, 75010 ☎ 01 46 07 34 50 Ⓜ La Chapelle

LA BOULE NOIRE/ LA CIGALE
www.laboule-noire.fr
www.lacigale.fr
Famous names have played at the diminutive La Boule Noire, in the heart of Pigalle, including Franz Ferdinand, Jamie Cullum and Metallica. It's linked to a former theatre, La Cigale, which hosts musicals, rock and pop, and music festivals.
✚ c2 ✉ 120 boulevard Rochechouart, 75018 ☎ 01 49 25 81 75 Ⓜ Pigalle, Anvers

DIVAN DU MONDE
www.divandumonde.com
The lower level of this former brothel is devoted to concerts of everything from rock to electronic and world music; the Divan Japonais upstairs holds theme evenings with DJs and video artists showing their talents.
✚ c3 ✉ 75 rue des Martyrs, 75018 ☎ 01 42 52 02 46 Ⓜ Pigalle

L'ELYSÉE-MONTMARTRE
www.elyseemontmartre.com
A concert venue in a building designed by Gustave Eiffel with mostly new rock groups. Also a club with regular theme evenings: rock, reggae, ballroom dancing.
✚ c2 ✉ 72 boulevard Rochechouart, 75018 ☎ 01 44 92 45 47 or 01 41 57 32 33 Ⓜ Anvers

FOLIE'S PIGALLE
This small club was once an Italian-style theatre, then a strip club. It has a different theme every evening and a gay tea dance on Sunday evening.
✚ b2 ✉ 11 place Pigalle, 75009 ☎ 01 48 78 55 25 ⏲ Mon–Sat midnight–6am, Sun 6pm–6am Ⓜ Pigalle

LA FOURMI
A great bar with retro furnishings and a funky bottle-rack chandelier. Young hip crowd.
✚ c2 ✉ 74 rue des Martyrs, 75018 ☎ 01 42 64 70 35 ⏲ Mon–Thu 8am–2am, Fri, Sat 8am–4am, Sun 10am–2am Ⓜ Pigalle

SO MUCH CHOICE

Paris has a huge number of wonderful bars and wine bars to choose from. These range from bars selling just beer, to cocktail and late-night bars dotted throughout the city. Most Parisian wine bars are small, neighbourly places, some selling food as well. You will find a great selection of regional wines. Explore the various areas to find a plethora of convivial drinking holes.

LA LOCO
www.laloco.com
Club with an industrial decor on three levels and different music styles (pop, house and R&B).
✚ b2 ✉ 90 boulevard de Clichy, 75009 ☎ 01 53 41 88 89 ⏲ Daily 11–dawn Ⓜ Blanche

MICHOU
www.michou.fr
A familiar sight in the district, Michou is always dressed in electric-blue suits and big eyeglasses. The drag show in this venerable club is still going strong.
✚ c2 ✉ 80 rue des Martyrs, 75018 ☎ 01 46 06 16 04 ⏲ Nightly dinner 8.30, show 10.45 Ⓜ Pigalle

MOULIN ROUGE
www.moulinrouge.fr
The 'Red Windmill', made famous by Toulouse-Lautrec, is the birthplace of the saucy cancan.
✚ b2 ✉ 82 boulevard de Clichy, 75018 ☎ 01 53 09 82 82 ⏲ Nightly dinner and show 7pm; show only 9 and 11 Ⓜ Blanche

STUDIO 28
The coolest cinema in Paris. Its new releases in the original language change every day or two, and it has its own little bar and garden. The crazy light fixtures in the screening room were designed by Jean Cocteau.
✚ b2 ✉ 10 rue Tholozé, 75018 ☎ 01 46 06 36 07 Ⓜ Abbesses, Blanche

Restaurants

PRICES

Prices are approximate, based on a 3-course meal for one person.

€€€ over €90
€€ €30–€90
€ under €30

AU CLAIR DE LA LUNE (€€)

Classically French cuisine is served in this comfortable, welcoming inn-style restaurant just off the place du Tertre. It's run by two brothers and is very popular with locals.
c1 9 rue Poulbot, 75018 01 42 58 97 03 Mon–Fri 12–2.30, 7–10.30, Sat 7–10.30 Abbesses

AU VIRAGE LEPIC (€–€€)

This welcoming bistro, in the heart of Montmartre, is well-known for its tasty meat-based main courses and delicious puddings, complemented by a great wine list. In summer you can sit outside.
b2 61 rue Lepic, 75018 01 42 52 46 79 Wed–Mon 7pm–11.30pm Blanche, Abbesses

BISTRO POULBOT (€€)

There's a fin-de-siècle setting at this celebrated eaterie on the Butte de Montmartre. The bistro gets rave reviews from diners from all over the world and has been recently renovated.
c1 39 rue Lamarck 75018 01 46 06 86 00 Mon–Sat 12–3, 7–10.30 Lamarck

CAFÉ BURQ (€€)

The crowd is young and the decor minimalist in this tiny Montmartre bistro, with a bar on one level and the dining room a few steps down. The food and wine are delicious and the service is pleasant.
b2 6 rue Burq, 75018 01 42 52 81 27 Mon–Sat dinner only Abbesses

CHEZ GRISETTE (€€)

A delightful little bistro with a female chef, Régine, who knows what's what in the kitchen. Her excellent cooking follows the seasons.
c2 14 rue Houdon, 75018 01 42 62 04 80 Mon–Fri dinner only Abbesses, Pigalle

LOCAL WINE

At the intersection of rue Saule and rue Saint-Vincent there is a small hillside of vines—a remnant of the former vineyards of the Butte Montmartre. During the wine harvest there is a very popular, colourful festival with plenty of tastings. For more information visit www.fetedesvendangesdemontmartre.com

CHEZ JEAN (€€€)

Solid comfort; creative dishes with fanciful names like Monsieur Cochon and Inspecteur Harry; friendly, professional service; and one Michelin star.
H2 8 rue Saint-Lazare, 75009 01 48 78 62 73 Mon–Fri lunch and dinner. Closed Aug Notre-Dame-de-Lorette, Trinité

LE PROGRÈS (€)

The kind of café where you'd expect to see a character from *Amélie*, which was filmed in the area. Animated staff and *plat du jour* at lunchtime.
c2 7 rue des Trois-Frères, 75018 01 42 64 07 37 Daily 9am–2am Abbesses

ROSE BAKERY (€)

A trendy English bakery and tea shop owned by a Franco-British couple. The food is organic. Popular for Sunday brunch.
c3 46 rue des Martyrs, 75009 01 42 82 12 80 Tue–Fri 9–7, Sat, Sun 10–5 Pigalle, Notre-Dame-de-Lorette

SOLE CAFFE & CUCINA (€€)

A trendy Italian restaurant with an attractive modern interior, complete with works of art, and very tasty cuisine. The coffee pannacotta is highly recommended for dessert.
d2 1 avenue Trudaine, 75009 01 42 81 11 34 Daily lunch and dinner Anvers

Some of the region's other attractions are well worth the trouble of getting there. Some, like Versailles, are not to be missed, while others, such as Père Lachaise or the Bois de Boulogne, offer a bucolic break.

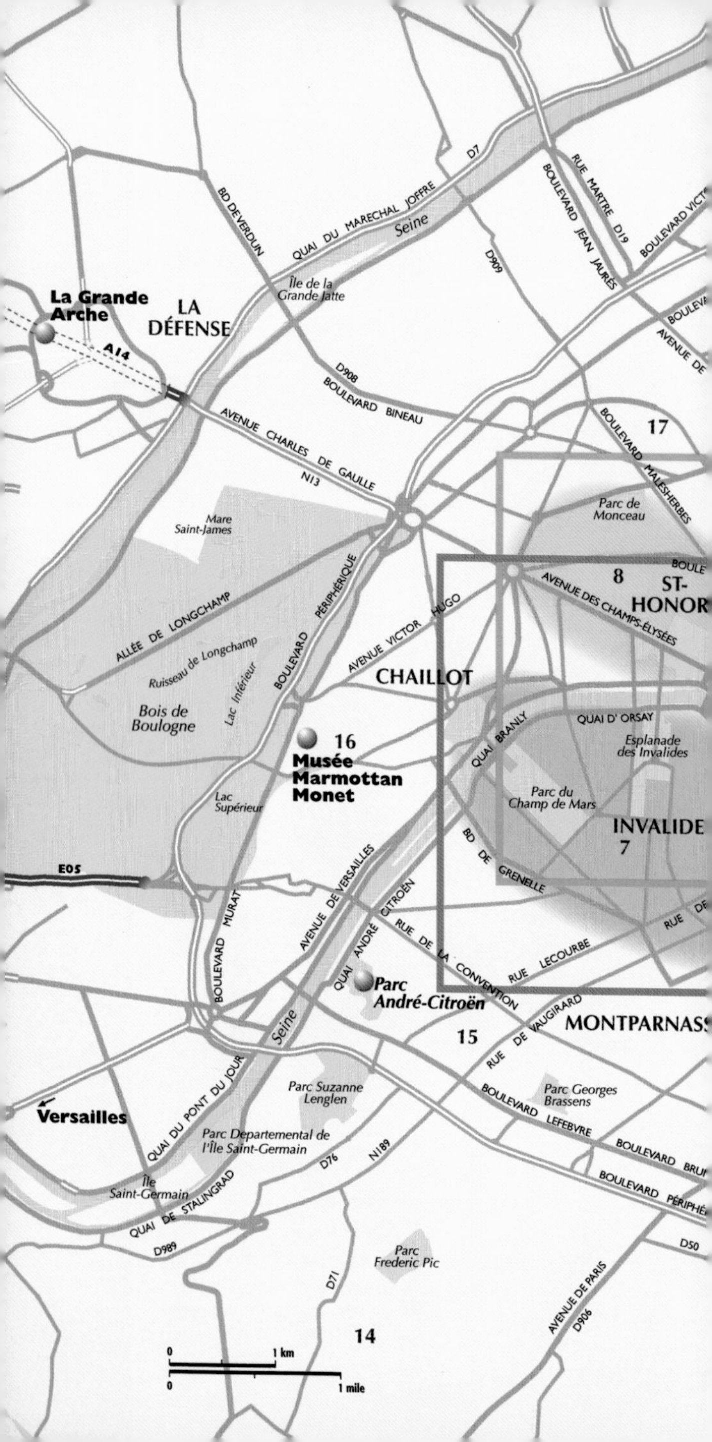

La Grande Arche
LA DÉFENSE
A14
BD DEVERDUN
QUAI DU MARECHAL JOFFRE
D7
Seine
Île de la Grande Jatte
D909
BOULEVARD JEAN JAURÈS
RUE MARTRE
D19
D908
BOULEVARD BINEAU
AVENUE CHARLES DE GAULLE
N13
BOULEVARD MALESHERBES
17
Parc de Monceau
Mare Saint-James
ALLÉE DE LONGCHAMP
Ruisseau de Longchamp
Lac Inférieur
Bois de Boulogne
BOULEVARD PÉRIPHÉRIQUE
AVENUE VICTOR HUGO
8
ST-HONOR
AVENUE DES CHAMPS-ÉLYSÉES
CHAILLOT
QUAI BRANLY
QUAI D' ORSAY
Esplanade des Invalides
16
Musée Marmottan Monet
Lac Supérieur
Parc du Champ de Mars
INVALIDE
7
BD DE GRENELLE
E05
BOULEVARD MURAT
AVENUE DE VERSAILLES
QUAI ANDRÉ CITROËN
RUE DE LA CONVENTION
RUE LECOURBE
Parc André-Citroën
MONTPARNASS
15
RUE DE VAUGIRARD
QUAI DU PONT DU JOUR
Parc Suzanne Lenglen
Parc Georges Brassens
Versailles
BOULEVARD LEFEBVRE
BOULEVARD BRU
Parc Departemental de l'Île Saint-Germain
D76
N189
Île Saint-Germain
QUAI DE STALINGRAD
BOULEVARD PÉRIPHÉ
D989
Parc Frederic Pic
D50
D71
AVENUE DE PARIS
D906
14
0
1 km
0
1 mile

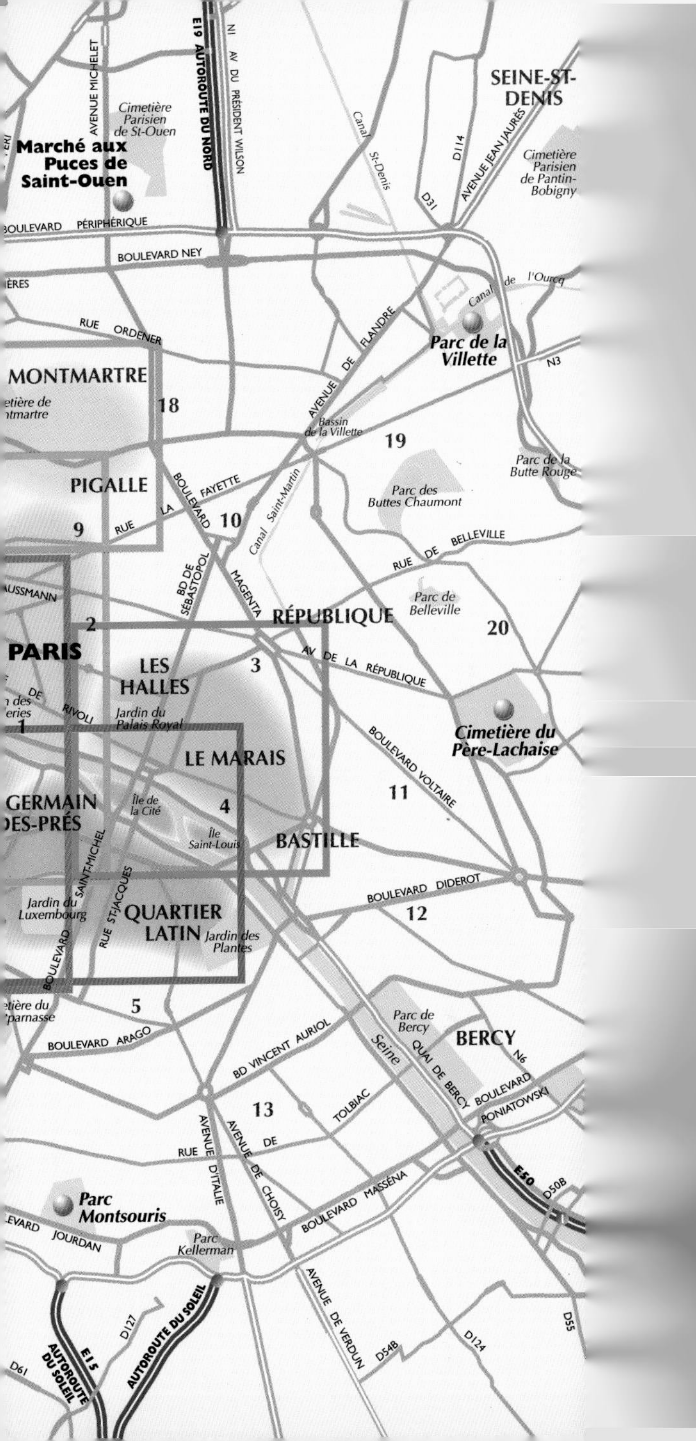

E19 AUTOROUTE DU NORD
N1 AV DU PRÉSIDENT WILSON
AVENUE MICHELET
Cimetière Parisien de St-Ouen
Marché aux Puces de Saint-Ouen
SEINE-ST-DENIS
D114
AVENUE JEAN JAURÈS
Cimetière Parisien de Pantin-Bobigny
D31
Canal St-Denis
BOULEVARD PÉRIPHÉRIQUE
BOULEVARD NEY
Canal de l'Ourcq
Parc de la Villette
N3
RUE ORDENER
MONTMARTRE
18
AVENUE DE FLANDRE
Bassin de la Villette
19
Parc de la Butte Rouge
PIGALLE
BOULEVARD
RUE LA FAYETTE
Canal Saint-Martin
Parc des Buttes Chaumont
9
10
RUE DE BELLEVILLE
BD DE SÉBASTOPOL
MAGENTA
Parc de Belleville
RÉPUBLIQUE
20
2
PARIS
LES HALLES
3
AV DE LA RÉPUBLIQUE
RIVOLI
Jardin du Palais Royal
1
Cimetière du Père-Lachaise
BOULEVARD VOLTAIRE
LE MARAIS
11
Île de la Cité
4
Île Saint-Louis
BASTILLE
SAINT-MICHEL
RUE ST-JACQUES
BOULEVARD DIDEROT
Jardin du Luxembourg
QUARTIER LATIN
Jardin des Plantes
12
BOULEVARD
5
Parc de Bercy
BERCY
Seine
QUAI DE BERCY
N6
BOULEVARD ARAGO
BD VINCENT AURIOL
BOULEVARD PONIATOWSKI
13
TOLBIAC
RUE DE
AVENUE D'ITALIE
AVENUE DE CHOISY
E50
D50B
Parc Montsouris
BOULEVARD MASSÉNA
JOURDAN
Parc Kellerman
AVENUE DE VERDUN
D127
AUTOROUTE DU SOLEIL
E15 AUTOROUTE DU SOLEIL
D54B
D124
D55
D61

Marché aux Puces de Saint-Ouen

Face masks (left) for sale at the market; antiques on display (right)

THE BASICS

www.parispuces.com
Off map
Porte de Clignancourt, 75018
0892 70 57 65
Sat–Mon 9–7 (until 5.30 in winter)
Cafés and restaurants on rue des Rosiers
Porte de Clignancourt
56, 85
Good
Free
Beware of pickpockets

HIGHLIGHTS

- Marché Serpette: art nouveau, antiques, painting
- Marché Paul Bert: antiques, quality bric-a-brac
- Marché Jules Vallès: bric-a-brac, furniture, prints
- Marché Biron: antiques, objets d'art
- Marché Vernaison: furniture and bric-a-brac
- Marché Cambo: paintings, furniture, objets d'art
- Marché Malik: second-hand clothes, accessories, ethnic goods

A Sunday pastime popular with many locals is to look for bargains at the city's flea markets, of which the *crème de la crème* is still this one. Nowhere else will you find such a fascinating cross-section of Parisian society.

Duck and banter The approach from the Métro station to this sprawling 7ha (17-acre) market is uninspiring as it entails bypassing household goods, jeans and shoe stalls before ducking under the Périphérique overpass and finally entering the fray. Persevere and you may discover an antique gem, a fake or a second-hand item. If your budget won't stretch to that you can choose an old postcard of Paris from the thousands on show. Everything and anything is displayed here but all commerce is carried on in the true bantering style of the *faubourgs*.

Bargain Registered dealers are divided into more than a dozen official markets, which interconnect through bustling passageways. Along the fringes are countless hopefuls who set up temporary stands to sell goods ranging from obsolete kitchenware to old jukeboxes and junk. Although unashamedly a tourist trap, there is something for everyone here, but do go early. Bargaining is obligatory. Stop for lunch in one of the bistros along the rue des Rosiers or try the terrace of A Picolo at 58 rue Jules-Vallès (jazz concerts on Sunday 6–8pm). On weekends as many as 150,000 bargain-hunters, tourists and dealers cram the passageways—avoid Sunday afternoons in particular.

The exterior (left) and interior (right) of the museum

TOP 25

Musée Marmottan Monet

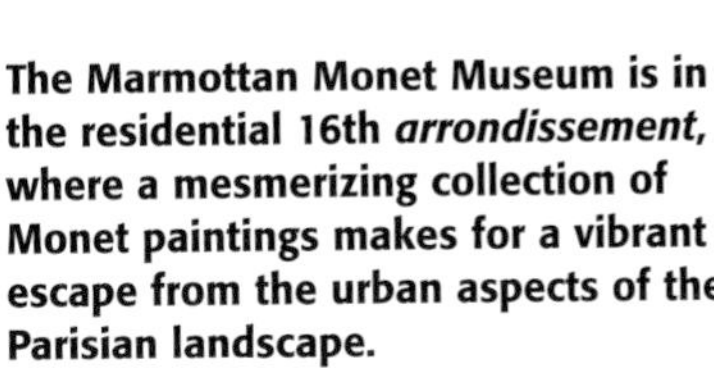

The Marmottan Monet Museum is in the residential 16th *arrondissement*, where a mesmerizing collection of Monet paintings makes for a vibrant escape from the urban aspects of the Parisian landscape.

Rich donations This often overlooked treasure of Parisian culture offers an eclectic collection built up over the years from the original donation of Renaissance and First Empire paintings and furniture given by the art historian Paul Marmottan in 1932. His elegant 19th-century mansion, furnished with Renaissance tapestries and sculptures and Napoleonic furniture, was later given an extra boost by the stunning Wildenstein collection of 313 pages from illustrated manuscripts from the 13th to the 16th centuries, as well as an exceptional donation from Michel Monet of works by his father Claude Monet, the Impressionist painter. Other generous donations include works by Monet's contemporaries Gauguin, Renoir, Pissarro, Sisley, Berthe Morisot and Gustave Caillebotte, but it is Monet's canvases of dappled irises, wisteria and water lilies, from his last years at Giverny, that are memorable.

Shame When nine major paintings were stolen from the Marmottan in 1985 it caused acute embarrassment, not least because the booty included Monet's *Impression–soleil levant*, which gave the art movement its name. Five years later the plundered paintings were discovered in Corsica and displayed once again.

THE BASICS

www.marmottan.com
Off map
2 rue Louis-Boilly, 75016
01 44 96 50 33
Tue 11–9, Wed–Sun 11–6 (last entry 30 mins before closing)
La Muette
22, 32, 52, 63
RER Line C, Boulainvilliers
Moderate

HIGHLIGHTS

- *Impression–soleil levant*, Monet
- *Bouquet de Fleurs*, Gauguin
- Gold table-tray
- Geographic clock
- *Promenade près d'Argenteuil*, Monet
- *Charing Cross Bridge*, Monet
- *L'Allée des Rosiers*, Monet
- *Le Pont Japonais*, Monet
- Monet's *Water Lilies* series
- Monet's spectacles

Père Lachaise

Edith Piaf's tomb (left) and the avenues (right) in the cemetery

THE BASICS

www.pere-lachaise.com
Off map
Boulevard de Ménilmontant/rue du Repos, 75020
01 55 25 82 10
Mid-Mar to early Nov Mon–Fri 8–6, Sat 8.30–6, Sun 9–6; Nov to mid-Mar Mon–Fri 8–5.30, Sat 8.30–5.30, Sun 9–5.30
Père Lachaise, Gambetta
60, 69, 102
Cobblestoned roads and hilly terrain
Free; tours moderate
Guided tours (English) see www.jardins.paris.fr or tel 01 40 71 75 60

HIGHLIGHTS

- Oscar Wilde's tomb
- Edith Piaf's tomb
- Chopin's tomb
- Marcel Proust's tomb
- Mur des Fédérés
- Delacroix's tomb
- Baron Haussmann's tomb
- Molière's tomb
- Jim Morrison's tomb

If you think cemeteries are lugubrious then a visit here may change your mind. The plethora of tomb designs, trees and twisting paths create a peaceful setting.

Pilgrimage This landscaped hillside, in the Ménilmontant district east of the heart of the city, is a popular haunt for rock fans, Piaf fans and lovers of poetry, literature, music and history. Since its creation in 1804 this vast cemetery has seen hundreds of the famous and illustrious buried within its precincts, so that a walk around its labyrinthine expanse presents a microcosm of French socio-cultural history. Pick up a map at the entrance or plot your visit in advance on the website.

Incumbents The cemetery was created in 1804 on Jesuit land where Louis XIV's confessor, Father La Chaise, once lived. It was the site of the Communards' tragic last stand in 1871, when the 147 survivors of a night-long fight met their bloody end in front of a government firing squad and were thrown into a communal grave, now commemorated by the Mur des Fédérés in the eastern corner. Memorials also commemorate victims of the Nazi concentration camps. Paths meander past striking funerary monuments and the graves of such well-known people as the star-crossed medieval lovers Abélard and Héloïse, painters Delacroix and Modigliani, actress Sarah Bernhardt, composers Poulenc and Bizet, and writers Balzac and Colette. Crowds of rock fans throng round the tomb of Jim Morrison, singer with The Doors, who died in Paris in 1971.

The Hall of Mirrors (left) and statues in the grounds (right)

TOP 25

Versailles

The Château de Versailles has undergone a massive renovation that has restored much of the grandeur enjoyed by the Sun King, Louis XIV.

A new palace Versailles is the ultimate symbol of French grandeur, and the backdrop to the death of the monarchy. After 1661, when Louis XIV assumed power, he announced his intention of moving his court to the site of his father's hunting lodge, where he created a royal residence, seat of government and home to French nobility. Building continued until his death in 1715, by which time the 100ha (247-acre) garden had been perfected by landscape garden designer André Le Nôtre.

Glorious gardens Hundreds of statues, follies and fountains (flowing weekends only, April to end of September), and the royal retreats of the Grand and Petit Trianon relieve the formal symmetry. There are also rowing boats, bicycles and a minitrain.

Highlights inside Visit the Grands Appartements (State apartments), with the staggeringly ornate Hall of Mirrors (its restoration was completed in June 2007). The Petits Appartements display France's most priceless examples of 18th-century decoration and may be visited by guided tour only. Don't miss Marie-Antoinette's delightful little farm, the Petit Trianon, where she liked to play at being a milkmaid. The Royal Opera reopened in 2009 after two years of renovation. It is the perfect example of a court theatre and is now welcoming back audiences for the new seasons.

THE BASICS

www.chateauversailles.fr

Off map

Place d'Armes, Versailles

01 30 83 78 00

State apartments Apr–end Oct Tue–Sun 9–6.30; Nov–end Mar Tue–Sun 9–5.30. Grand and Petit Trianon daily 12–5.30 (until 6.30 in summer). Park daily 7am–8.30pm (until 6 in winter). Fountains Apr–end Sep Sat, Sun 11–12, 3.30–5

171

RER C, Versailles Rive Gauche

Few (State apartments)

Château moderate (visitors with disabilities free); park free; garden free Oct–end Mar, moderate Apr–end Sep. (If you already have tickets, go to the A access. If not, go to the Ticket Information point, South Ministers' Wing

Guided tour

HIGHLIGHTS

- Hall of Mirrors
- Petit Trianon
- Formal gardens
- Grandes Eaux

More to See

LA GRANDE ARCHE

www.grandearche.com

A marble window on the world designed by Johann Otto von Spreckelsen for the 1989 Bicentennial. Take the exterior elevator for views along the city's historical La Défense–Arc de Triomphe–Louvre axis.

Off map · 1 Parvis de La Défense · 01 49 07 27 55 · Daily 10–7 (until 8pm Apr–end Sep); ticket office closes 30 mins earlier · Grande Arche de la Défense · Moderate

PARC ANDRÉ-CITROËN

A cool futurist 1990s park divided into specialist gardens, on the site of a former Citroën factory. You'll find zany experimentation with metal and water.

Off map · Rue Balard, rue Leblanc, 75015 · Mon–Fri 8–dusk, Sat, Sun 9–dusk · Balard, Javel · Free

PARC MONTSOURIS

A Haussmann creation designed on English models, with copses, serpentine paths, play areas and a small lake with a waterfall.

Off map · Avenue Reille or boulevard Jourdan, 75014 · Mon–Fri 8–dusk, Sat, Sun 9–dusk · Restaurant · RER Line B, Cité Universitaire · Free

PARC DE LA VILLETTE

www.villette.com

The ultramodern Parc de la Villette, Paris's largest green space, catapults you into a futuristic world with a range of cultural and leisure activities. There's a science museum, music complex, hemispheric cinema, exhibition venue and concert hall. A covered walkway runs the length of the park, linking the Cité de Sciences et de l'Industrie and Cité de la Musique. At the Musée de la Musique nearly 1,000 musical instruments are showcased, dating from the Renaissance onwards.

Off map · Park: 211 avenue Jean-Jaurès; Cité des Sciences: 30 avenue Corentin-Cariou, 75019 · Park: 01 40 03 75 75; Cité des Sciences: 01 40 05 80 00 · Cité des Sciences: Tue–Sat 10–6, Sun 10–7 · Cafés, restaurants · Park: Porte de Pantin; Cité des Sciences: Porte de la Villette · Park: free; Cité des Sciences: moderate · Reserve shows, films and activities as soon as you arrive

La Grande Arche

Parc de la Villette

Excursions

BOIS DE BOULOGNE

An area of 845ha (2,090 acres), with 600 wild plant species, and many kilometres of horse-riding trails and biking paths. Oak trees cover over half the park. Distractions range from boating to clay-pigeon shooting and gastronomy. The Jardin d'Acclimatation is good for children, with playgrounds, minigolf, puppet shows, a toy train and the 'Explor@dome'.

THE BASICS

- Off map
- Permanently open, but avoid at night
- Cafés, restaurants
- Porte Dauphine, Porte d'Auteuil

CHANTILLY

The Château de Chantilly is one of the most picturesque castles in the region. It is surrounded by attractive parkland, with the forest of Chantilly beyond, and contains a magnificent art collection. The town of Chantilly is one of the leading training venues in Europe for racehorses and is home to a world-famous racecourse and the Musée Vivant du Cheval horse museum.

THE BASICS

www.chateaudechantilly.com
- Off map
- 03 44 62 62 62
- Apr–end Oct Wed–Mon 10–6; Nov–end Mar 10.30–5
- Chantilly-Gouvieux

DISNEYLAND RESORT PARIS

Disneyland Resort Paris attracts millions of visitors to its two Parks—Disneyland Park and Walt Disney Studios Park. The resort, in the Marne-la-Vallée countryside east of Paris, opened in 1992. The Walt Disney Studios Park was added in 2002. Other attractions include the Disney Village entertainment complex, eight hotels and even a golf course.

THE BASICS

www.disneylandparis.com
- Off map
- BP 100, Marne-la-Vallée, 77777, Cedex 4
- 01 60 30 60 30
- RER Line A, Marne-la-Vallée

FONTAINEBLEAU

Fontainebleau has witnessed momentous events, including the birth of Louis XIII in 1601 and Napoleon signing his deed of abdication in 1814. As far back as the 12th century kings went hunting in the forest. The keep in the Oval Courtyard is the only remnant of a medieval castle.

THE BASICS

www.musee-chateau-fontainebleau.fr
- Off map
- 01 60 71 50 70/60
- Fontainebleau-Avon

Restaurants

PRICES

Prices are approximate, based on a 3-course meal for one person.

€€€	over €90
€€	€30–€90
€	under €30

LA CAPITAINERIE (€–€€)
Inside the Château de Chantilly, in the former kitchens of Vatel, inventor of Chantilly cream and chef to Louis XIV. Serves brasserie-style food, with a buffet on weekends and tea in the afternoon.
✉ Château de Chantilly
☎ 03 44 57 15 89
🕐 Wed–Mon lunch only
🚆 Chantilly–Gouvieux

CHALET DES ÎLES (€€)
The only way to get to this big chalet-style restaurant (seats 100), on an island on one of the Bois de Boulogne lakes, is by a small ferryboat. Enjoy traditional French food. A fireplace and piano player in winter create a warm ambience.
✉ Bois de Boulogne Lac Inférieur, 75016 ☎ 01 42 88 04 69 🕐 Summer daily lunch, dinner; winter Tue–Sat lunch, dinner, Sun lunch only
🚇 Rue de la Pompe

CROQUEMBOUCHE (€€)
A pleasant spot in the heart of Fontainebleau for a traditional French meal.
✉ 43 rue de France, 77300 Fontainebleau ☎ 01 64 22 01 57 🕐 Tue–Fri lunch, dinner, Sat, Mon dinner
🚆 Fontainebleau–Avon

LA GRANDE CASCADE (€€€)
Napoleon III built this pavilion at the foot of La Grande Cascade (the Great Waterfall) for his visits to the Bois de Boulogne. It became a restaurant in 1900. The windows in the circular dining room give magical views of the woods. The Michelin-starred chef, Frédéric Robert, creates fine French cuisine.
✉ Allée de Longchamp, Bois de Boulogne, 75016 ☎ 01 45 27 33 51 🕐 Daily lunch, dinner 🚇 Porte Maillot, then bus 244

LA GUINGUETTE DE NEUILLY (€€)
Dine on the banks of the Seine on the Île de la Grande Jatte. The cuisine is simple but tasty, with choices such as grilled steak or roasted sea bass.
✉ 12 boulevard Georges-Seurat, 92200 Neuilly ☎ 01 46 24 25 04 🕐 Daily lunch, dinner 🚇 Pont de Levallois or Porte de Champerret then bus 163 or 164

PICNIC LUNCHES

If your taste is for a *déjeuner sur l'herbe* in Fontainebleau, the rue Grande grocery shops are perfect for picnic supplies. In Versailles, the Marché Notre-Dame is an excellent covered market (closed on Mondays) for stocking up on lunch items. When in Chantilly, allow yourself to be tempted by the patisseries, with their delicious cakes and pastries, with lashings of the eponymous cream.

LA MÈRE LACHAISE (€€)
After a visit to Père Lachaise cemetery, have a meal in this lively, trendy restaurant serving French specialities. A popular brunch is served on weekends.
✉ 78 boulevard de Ménilmontant, 75020 ☎ 01 47 97 61 60 🕐 Daily lunch and dinner 🚇 Père Lachaise

PRÉ CATALAN (€€€)
This three-star Michelin restaurant offers highly refined cuisine in a spectacular garden setting in the Bois de Boulogne. Ideal for a romantic summer evening. The chef is Frédéric Anton.
✉ Route de Suresnes, Bois de Boulogne, 75016 ☎ 01 44 14 41 14 🕐 Tue–Sat lunch and dinner, Sun lunch in summer
🚇 Porte Maillot then taxi

LE SOLEIL (€–€€)
The interior may be made up of flea-market finds, but the cuisine is fresh and delicious. There are occasional jazz concerts on weekends.
✉ 109 avenue Michelet, 93400 Saint-Ouen ☎ 01 40 10 08 08 🕐 Daily lunch only
🚇 Porte de Clignancourt

Where to Stay

Hip, chic, charming or cheap, Paris has the whole range of accommodation options. The city is still among the most affordable and most characterful of European capitals when it comes to finding a hotel.

Staying in Paris

The city's hotels have had a (sometimes deserved) reputation for being dated and uncomfortably small, but recent years have seen a complete overhaul. Boutique hotels have sprung up all over the city, especially in the Marais. Hotels around the Louvre, Champs-Élysées and Opéra tend to be more expensive, while those in the Latin Quarter are often smaller and more affordable.

Finding a good deal

Some of the luxury hotels are out of another era. Their stated prices are high but some give discounts through travel agents so it is worth asking. Paris is one of the rare European capitals where you can find a pleasant, affordable place to stay in a central part of the city. The Paris Tourist Office (▷ 118) has information. You can reserve rooms if you visit in person.

Helpful Tips

Prices often drop in July and August and rise in May, June, September and October—the trade fair months. Check whether the price includes breakfast. If you are bringing or renting a car, ask whether parking is available and how much it costs. Parking on the street can be expensive and frustrating.

Outer Limits

Chain hotels on the outskirts can be less expensive, but they lack character. You'll also have to spend more time taking the Métro.

APARTMENT LIVING

- To rent an apartment, options include the UK-based Apartment Service (tel 020 8944 1444 from the UK; 011 44 20 8944 1444 from the US; www.apartment.co.uk); Home Rental Service at 120 avenue des Champs-Élysées, 75008 (tel 01 42 25 65 40; www.homerental. fr); and Paris Lodging at 25 rue Lacépède, 75005 (tel 01 43 36 71 69; www.parislodging.fr).
- For bed-and-breakfast accommodation try France Lodge at 2 rue Meissonnier, 75017 (tel 01 56 33 85 80).

Budget Hotels

PRICES

Expect to pay between €50 and €150 for a budget hotel

GRAND HÔTEL MALHER

www.grandhotelmalher.com

Family hotel with 31 well-equipped rooms; excellent location.

L6 ✉ 5 rue Malher, 75004 (Marais) ☎ 01 42 72 60 92; fax 01 42 72 25 37 Ⓜ St-Paul

HÔTEL DE L'AVRE

www.hoteldelavre.com

Minutes from the Eiffel Tower, an impeccably kept two-star hotel. Breakfast is served in the pretty garden in spring and summer. 26 rooms.

B8 ✉ 21 rue de l'Avre, 75015 (Champs de Mars) ☎ 01 45 75 31 03; fax 01 45 75 63 26 Ⓜ La Motte-Picquet Grenelle

BUDGET HOTELS

Gone are the heady days when Paris was peppered with atmospheric basic hotels with their inimitable signs '*eau à tous les étages*' (water on every floor). Now there are usually bath or shower rooms with every bedroom, resulting in higher prices and smaller rooms. So don't expect much space in budget hotel rooms, but do expect breakfast and receptionists who speak a second language in hotels with two or more stars.

HÔTEL BELLEVUE & DU CHARIOT D'OR

www.hotelbellevue75.com

Dating from the mid-19th century, the hotel's grand Haussmann-style facade belies the simple bedrooms within. But this two-star place is comfortable and very good value, located just north of the Pompidou Centre and close to the Forum des Halles. All rooms are en suite and there is a lift.

K4 ✉ 39 rue de Turbigo, 75003 (Marais) ☎ 01 48 87 45 60; fax 01 48 87 95 04 Ⓜ Châtelet–Les Halles, Réaumur-Sebastopol

HÔTEL DU COLLÈGE DE FRANCE

www.hotel-collegedefrance.com

Tranquil 29-room hotel near the Sorbonne.

J7 ✉ 7 rue Thénard, 75005 (Quartier Latin) ☎ 01 43 26 78 36; fax 01 46 34 58 29 Ⓜ Maubert–Mutualité

HÔTEL DE LA PLACE DES VOSGES

www.hotelplacedesvosges.com

Lovely 17th-century town house in a quiet street. Basic comforts; excellent location. 16 rooms.

M6 ✉ 12 rue de Birague, 75004 (Marais/Bastille) ☎ 01 42 72 60 46; fax 01 42 72 02 64 Ⓜ Bastille, Saint-Paul

HÔTEL PRIMA LEPIC

www.hotel-paris-lepic.com

This two-star hotel is near Sacré-Cœur. The brightly painted bedrooms have been carefully furnished, and five have canopy beds. Each has a TV, hairdryer and modem connection.

b2 ✉ 29 rue Lepic, 75018 (Montmartre) ☎ 01 46 06 44 64 Ⓜ Blanche, Abbesses

TIMHOTEL MONTMARTRE

www.timhotel.com

On the charming, tree-shaded place Emile Goudeau, this pleasant hotel has the rare advantage of panoramic views of Paris from some rooms on its upper floors.

b2 ✉ 11 rue Ravignan, 75018 (Montmartre) ☎ 01 42 55 74 79; fax 01 42 55 71 01 Ⓜ Abbesses

TIMHOTEL QUARTIER LATIN JARDIN DES PLANTES

www.timhotel.com

Pretty 33-room hotel overlooking the botanical gardens.

K8 ✉ 5 rue Linné, 75005 (Latin Quarter) ☎ 01 47 07 06 20; fax 01 47 07 62 74 Ⓜ Jussieu

YOUTH HOSTELS

One way of seeing Paris on a budget is to stay in a youth hostel. Try the Auberge Internationale des Jeunes (10 rue Trousseau, 75011; tel 01 47 00 62 00; fax 01 47 00 33 16; www.aijparis.com), which offers shared rooms in the lively Bastille area at rock-bottom prices. Don't expect anything fancy, but the atmosphere is friendly. There are 200 beds in rooms for 2, 3 or 4 people.

Mid-Range Hotels

PRICES

Expect to pay between €150 and €250 for a mid-range hotel

THE FIVE HOTEL

www.thefivehotel.com

Tiny rooms but plenty of designer punch in this hotel, opened in 2006 on a quiet street. The 23 bright rooms are scented with the heavenly fragrances of Diptyque and boast fun lighting effects and original artwork.

J9 3 rue Flatters, 75005 01 43 31 73 21; fax 01 43 31 61 96 Gobelins

HÔTEL DE L'ABBAYE SAINT-GERMAIN

www.hotel-abbaye.com

This quaint, historic hotel was once a convent. The lounge and most of the 44 rooms look out onto a patio. Eight suites, some with private terrace.

G7 10 rue Cassette, 75006 (Saint-Sulpice) 01 45 44 38 11; fax 01 45 48 07 86 Saint-Sulpice

HÔTEL D'ANGLETERRE

www.hotel-dangleterre.com

Former 18th-century British embassy. Garden patio, 27 spacious rooms. Hemingway once lived here. Bar and piano lounge.

G6 44 rue Jacob, 75006 (Saint-Germain-des-Prés) 01 42 60 34 72; fax 01 42 60 16 93 Saint-Germain-des-Prés

HÔTEL ATLANTIS SAINT-GERMAIN-DES-PRÉS

www.hotelatlantis.com

Most of the 27 bright and airy rooms face onto pretty place Saint-Sulpice. All have been beautifully decorated, and have good facilities. The communal areas are elegant.

G7 4 rue du Vieux-Colombier, 75006 01 45 48 31 81; fax 01 45 48 35 16 Saint-Sulpice

HÔTEL DESIGN DE LA SORBONNE

www.hotelsorbonne.com

This newly renovated hotel has contemporary living down to a fine art. Each floor has photos, engravings and literary quotes that complement the British-style decor. The 38 bedrooms have iMac computers, among the opulent facilities.

H8 6 rue Victor-Cousin, 75005 01 43 54 58 08; fax 01 40 51 05 18 Cluny–La Sorbonne

MID-RANGE HOTELS

All these mid-priced establishments are popular with business visitors, so it is virtually impossible to find rooms during trade-fair seasons such as May to early June and mid-September to October. In summer many offer discounts as their clientele shrinks. All rooms are equipped with TV, phone, private bath or shower rooms, minibar and most with hairdryer. Air-conditioning is not standard, but elevators are common.

HÔTEL DUC DE SAINT-SIMON

www.hotelducdesaintsimon.com

Rather pricey (at the top end of mid-range) but the antiques and picturesque setting just off boulevard Saint-Germain justify it. 34 comfortable rooms, and an intimate atmosphere. Reserve far ahead.

F6 14 rue Saint-Simon, 75007 (Saint-Germain-des-Prés) 01 44 39 20 20; fax 01 45 48 68 25 Rue du Bac

HÔTEL LAUTREC OPÉRA

www.paris-hotel-lautrec.com

This three-star hotel is named after the artist Henri Toulouse-Lautrec, who once lived here. It is classified as a historic monument and has a beautiful 18th-century facade. Inside, there's a more contemporary feel, with pale wood furniture and blue-and-yellow upholstery; some rooms have exposed bricks and beams and all have satellite TV.

H3 8–10 rue d'Amboise, 75002 (Opéra) 01 42 96 67 90 Richelieu-Drouot

HÔTEL LENOX SAINT-GERMAIN

www.lenoxsaintgermain.com

Popular with the design and fashion world. Chase T. S. Eliot's ghost and

enjoy the restored, stylish 1930s bar. 34 rooms.
G6 9 rue de l'Université, 75007 (Saint-Germain-des-Prés) 01 42 96 10 95; fax 01 42 61 52 83 Saint-Germain-des-Prés

HÔTEL DES MARRONNIERS

www.hotel-marronniers.com
Oak-beamed rooms and vaulted cellars are converted to lounges. Ask for a room overlooking the garden. 37 rooms.
G6 21 rue Jacob, 75006 (Saint-Germain-des-Prés) 01 43 25 30 60; fax 01 40 46 83 56 Saint-Germain-des-Prés

HÔTEL MOLIÈRE

www.hotel-moliere.fr
On a quiet street near the Louvre and Opéra. 32 clean, reasonably priced rooms. No restaurant.
G4 21 rue Molière, 75001 (Opéra) 01 42 96 22 01; fax 01 42 60 48 68 Pyramides, Palais-Royal

HÔTEL LA PERLE

www.hotellaperle.com
Renovated 18th-century building on a quiet street near Saint-Germain. 38 rooms.
G7 14 rue des Canettes, 75006 (Saint-Germain-des-Prés) 01 43 29 10 10; fax 01 46 34 51 04 Mabillon

HÔTEL RÉCAMIER

www.hotelrecamier.com
Tranquil, friendly little hotel close to Saint-Germain and the Luxembourg gardens. There are 24 beautifully renovated rooms.
G7 3 bis place Saint-Sulpice, 75006 (Saint-Germain-des-Prés) 01 43 26 04 89; fax 01 46 33 27 73 Saint-Sulpice

HOTEL RÉSIDENCE FOCH

www.foch-paris-hotel.com
Charming three-star hotel with elegantly furnished rooms filled with good quality furniture and traditional French touches. There's a bright bar on the ground floor and a private courtyard garden where you can relax over breakfast or a drink.
Off map at A3 10 rue Marbeau, 75116 (Champs-Élysées) 01 45 00 46 50; fax 01 45 01 98 68 Porte Dauphine

HÔTEL SAINTE-BEUVE

www.parishotelcharme.com
Exclusive hotel between Montparnasse and the Luxembourg gardens. Period antiques and modern furnishings. 22 rooms.
G8 9 rue Sainte-Beuve, 75006 01 45 48 20 07; fax 01 45 48 67 52 Notre-Dame-des-Champs

BED-AND-BREAKFAST

Paris is trying to increase its small stock of bed-and-breakfasts by encouraging residents to open up their homes to visitors and establishing standards for B&Bs. If you'd like to stay with a French host, the following organizations can help you: Alcôve & Agapes: www.parisbb.com; Association Française BAB France: www.babfrance.fr; Fleurs de Soleil: www.fleursdesoleil.fr

HÔTEL DE L'UNIVERSITÉ

www.paris-hotel-universite.com
A Left Bank hotel par excellence, with its individually decorated rooms (27), some with (non-working) fireplaces, antique furnishings and exposed beams.
G6 22 rue de l'Université, 75007 (Saint-Germain-des-Prés) 01 42 61 09 39; fax 01 42 60 40 84 Rue du Bac

RÉSIDENCE LORD BYRON

www.hotel-lordbyron.fr
Comfortable, classy 31-room hotel just off the Champs-Élysées. Small garden.
C2 5 rue Châteaubriand, 75008 (Champs-Élysées) 01 43 59 89 98; fax 01 42 89 46 04 Georges V

LES RIVES DE NOTRE-DAME

www.rivesdenotredame.com
Overlooking the banks of the Seine, this hotel has beamed ceilings, marble tiling, tapestries and fine wrought-iron furniture. 10 rooms, 1 suite.
J7 15 quai Saint-Michel, 75005 (Latin Quarter) 01 43 54 81 16; fax 01 43 26 27 09 Saint-Michel

Luxury Hotels

PRICES

Expect to pay between €250 and €800 for a luxury hotel

L'HÔTEL

www.l-hotel.com

A Parisian legend that is exuberantly elegant and intimate. Oscar Wilde stayed here and celebrities are often to be found in the discreet bar. Restaurant and some superb rooms. 20 rooms.

G6 13 rue des Beaux-Arts, 75006 (Saint-Germain-des-Prés) 01 44 41 99 00; fax 01 43 25 64 81 Saint-Germain-des-Prés

HÔTEL LE BELLECHASSE

www.lebellechasse.com

If you like Christian Lacroix's clothing, with plenty of colours and prints, you'll love this elegant Left Bank hotel, which has been entirely redecorated by the fashion designer. Each of the 34 rooms sports one of seven themes, among them 'Avengers', 'Tuileries', 'Musqueteers' and 'Patchwork'.

F5 8 rue de Bellechasse, 75007 01 45 50 22 31; fax 01 45 51 52 36 Solferino

HÔTEL DE CRILLON

www.crillon.com

Fabulous Parisian classic that reeks glamour, style, history and major investments. 119 rooms plus 28 suites.

E4 10 place de la Concorde, 75008 (Concorde/ Champs-Élysées) 01 44 71 15 00; fax 01 44 71 15 02 Concorde

HÔTEL DU JEU DE PAUME

www.jeudepaumehotel.com

A small, delightful hotel carved out of a 17th-century royal tennis court. 28 tasteful rooms with beams and marble bathrooms; some suites. No restaurant.

K7 54 rue Saint-Louis-en-l'Île, 75004 (Île Saint-Louis) 01 43 26 14 18; fax 01 40 46 02 76 Pont Marie

HÔTEL MONTALEMBERT

www.montalembert.com

A fashionable Left Bank hotel with a garden-patio, bar and restaurant. Chic design details and 56 well-appointed rooms and 7 suites.

F6 3 rue de Montalembert, 75007 (Saint-Germain-des-Prés) 01 45 49 68 68; fax 01 45 49 69 49 Rue du Bac

LE CRILLON

Whether you stay at the Ritz, the Crillon, the Meurice, the Bristol or the Georges V, they all have their tales to tell, but that of the Crillon (▷ left) is perhaps the most momentous. This mansion managed to survive the Revolution despite having the guillotine on its doorstep. Mary Pickford and Douglas Fairbanks spent their honeymoon here.

HÔTEL SAN RÉGIS

www.hotel-sanregis.fr

Elaborately decorated hotel; popular with showbiz folk. 41 rooms and 3 suites.

D4 12 rue Jean-Goujon, 75008 (Champs-Élysées) 01 44 95 16 16; fax 01 45 61 05 48 Franklin D. Roosevelt, Champs-Élysées–Clémenceau

MURANO URBAN RESORT

www.muranoresort.com

Sharp modern design, variable lighting effects and great attention to detail characterize this trendy hotel with a highly popular bar and new covered terrace. In an up-and-coming area near the place de la République. In-house restaurant. 49 rooms and 2 suites.

M4 13 boulevard du Temple, 75003 01 42 71 20 00; fax 01 42 71 21 01 République, Filles du Calvaire

PAVILLON DE LA REINE

www.pavillon-de-la-reine.com

Period decoration and lavish furnishings in this 17th-century building are enhanced by the flowery courtyard and a lovely leafy garden. No restaurant. 41 rooms, 16 suites.

M6 28 place des Vosges, 75003 (Marais) 01 40 29 19 19; fax 01 40 29 19 20 Bastille

Use this section to familiarize yourself with travel to and within Paris. The Essential Facts will give you insider knowledge of the city.

Planning Ahead

When to Go

Spring is a popular time, with its lovely chestnut blossoms. The city reaches peak tourist capacity in hot, sunny July. However, with the Parisian exodus to the countryside in August the city is emptier than usual. Autumn is busy with trade fairs and rooms can be scarce and expensive.

TIME

Paris is one hour ahead of London, six hours ahead of New York and nine hours ahead of Los Angeles.

AVERAGE DAILY MAXIMUM TEMPERATURES

JAN	FEB	MAR	APR	MAY	JUN	JUL	AUG	SEP	OCT	NOV	DEC
6°C	7°C	12°C	16°C	20°C	23°C	25°C	26°C	21°C	16°C	10°C	7°C
43°F	45°F	54°F	61°F	68°F	73°F	77°F	79°F	70°F	61°F	50°F	45°F

Spring (April, May) takes time to get going. Things don't usually warm up until mid-May.
Summer (June to August) can be glorious. Days are longest in June, with the most sunshine and a pleasant temperature. Hot and sunny in July, it is often hot, humid and stormy in August.
Autumn (September to November) has crisp days and usually clear skies.
Winter (December to March) is rarely below freezing but it rains frequently, sometimes with hail, in January and March.

WHAT'S ON

January/February *Chinese New Year*: In Chinatown.
April/May *International Paris Fair*: Consumer heaven at Porte de Versailles; www.foiredeparis.fr.
Paris marathon: Starts from the Champs-Élysées; www.parismarathon.com.
May *Labour Day* (1 May): Parades and symbolic lily-of-the-valley bouquets.
La Nuit des Musées: On one Saturday evening museums fling their doors open with music, drama and readings.
June *Foire Saint-Germain*: Cultural fair at place Saint-Sulpice.
Fête de la Musique (21 Jun): Music on the streets.
Course des Garçons de Café (late Jun): Waiters and waitresses race through the streets, armed with tray, bottle and glasses.
July *Bastille Day* (14 Jul): The most important French festival celebrates the 1789 storming of the Bastille. Fireworks and street dances on the evening of the 13th and a parade on the 14th on the Champs-Élysées.
July–August *Paris Quartier d'Été*: Outdoor performances; www.quartierdete.com.
Paris Plage: A beach along the quays of the Seine on the Right Bank.
September *Festival d'Automne à Paris* (mid-Sep to end Dec): Music, theatre and dance all over the city; www.festival-automne.com.
October *Foire Internationale d'Art Contemporain*: Paris's biggest modern art fair; www.fiacparis.com.
Nuit Blanche: For one night various cultural venues open all night, free of charge.
November *Beaujolais Nouveau* (third Thu in Nov): Drinking in all the city's bars.
December *Paris International Boat Show*.

Useful Websites

www.paris-ile-de-france.com or www.pidf.com
The website of the Paris Île de France regional tourist authority has a huge quantity and variety of information on Paris and the surrounding region, including entertainment and events, shopping, sport and leisure, children's Paris, accommodation and public transport.

www.parisinfo.com
The Paris Tourist Office online, with listings and practical information, sightseeing and links to other useful sites covering every aspect of leisure in the city. Browse a selection of the week's events or check out an air-quality report. There's also online hotel booking.

www.parisfranceguide.com
This site, aimed at English-speakers, is about getting orientated in Paris and finding what you are looking for–a job and an apartment, a hotel or events information.

www.parisvoice.com
Click here and you'll feel like you're already in the city. Intended for English-speaking Parisians, it gives an insider's view of the city, with features, events information, restaurant reviews, classified ads, a Q&A column (dealing with some very serious issues) and more.

www.paris.fr
The official site of Paris's mayor and city council has information on museums, theatres, parks and sport, as well as a virtual tour of the Hôtel de Ville. There is also a wealth of civic news aimed at Paris residents.

www.parissi.com
Look up this website for Paris disco, dance and clubland news (French only).

www.paris-update.com
What's happening, updated weekly: art shows, films, restaurants, concerts.

PRIME TRAVEL SITES

www.parisdigest.com
Independent city guide showing you around the city and providing a huge quantity of mainstream practical information. A good range of hotel, restaurant and shopping guides.

www.fodors.com
A complete travel-planning site. You can research prices and weather; book air tickets, cars and rooms; ask questions (and get answers) from fellow travellers; and find links to other sites.

INTERNET CAFÉS

Web 46
K9 · 46 rue de Roi de Sicile, 75004 · 01 40 27 02 89 · Mon–Fri 9.30am–10.30pm, Sat 9.30–9, Sun 11–10.30 · Hôtel de Ville

Actuel Bureautique
K9 · 14 rue Santeuil, 75005 · 08 70 71 41 03 · Mon–Fri 9.15–7 · Censier-Daubenton

La Baguenaude
J5 · 30 rue de la Grande Truanderie, 75001 · 01 40 26 27 74 · Mon–Sat 10–8.45 (also Sun Apr–end Nov) · Châtelet, Etienne-Marcel

Getting There

GETTING YOUR BEARINGS

Think of Paris as a snail, with its shell curling around the 1st *arrondissement* (district) right in the middle. The numbers of the other *arrondissements* follow clockwise, ending with the 20th on the eastern side of the city. *C'est logique, non?*

TIPPING

In every restaurant, by law, a 15 per cent service charge and all relevant taxes are already in the prices on the menu. If the service was especially pleasant, or if you feel odd about leaving nothing, then you can leave another couple of euros or 5 per cent. In taxis it is customary to give the driver a 10 per cent tip, but only if you are happy with the service.

AIRPORTS

Most international flights arrive at Roissy Charles de Gaulle airport, with some international and French domestic flights arriving at Orly airport. Paris has good rail connections, including the Eurostar train direct from London.

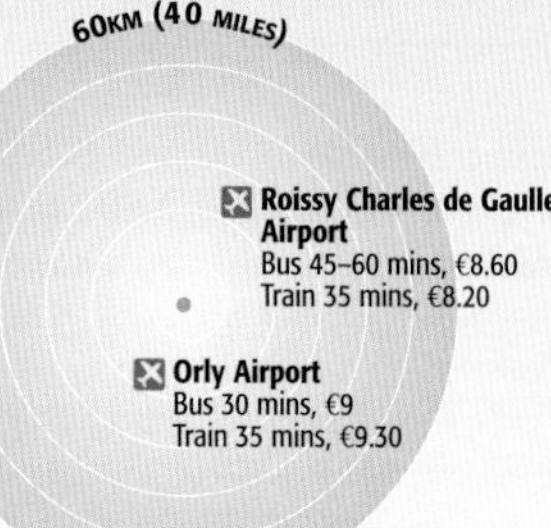

FROM ROISSY CHARLES DE GAULLE

Roissy (☎ 3950; outside France 331 70 36 39 50; www.adp.fr) is 23km (14 miles) northeast of central Paris and has three terminals. Air France currently operates out of Terminal 2. There are three ways to get to the city. By bus: Air France (www.cars-airfrance.com) operates a bus service between the airport and Montparnasse and Gare

de Lyon, every 30 minutes 7am–9pm (€14), and to the Arc de Triomphe and Porte Maillot every 15 minutes, 5.45am–11pm (€13). Or take the 50-minute trip on Roissybus that runs every 15 or 20 minutes from Terminals 1, 2 and 3 to Opéra 6am–11pm (€8.60). By train: A surburban train network, the RER (Réseau Express Régional) takes around 35 minutes to central Paris (€8.20). Trains leave every 10–15 minutes. By taxi: A taxi costs around €50 (confirm the price with the driver before setting off) and takes between 30 minutes and 1 hour, depending on traffic.

FROM ORLY

Orly (☎ 3950; outside France 331 70 36 39 50; www.adp.fr), the older and smaller of Paris's two main international airports, is 14km (8.5 miles) south of central Paris with no direct public transport links. By bus: Air France provides shuttle buses to Les Invalides and Gare Montparnasse every 15 minutes 6am–11.30pm (€9). The trip takes about 30 minutes. By train: The Orlyval train, which operates daily 6am–11pm, will take you to Antony, where you can change for line B of the main Paris RER rail system (€9.30). From here it's around 30 minutes to central Paris. By taxi: A taxi costs around €40 (confirm the price before setting off) and takes 15–30 minutes.

BUDGET OPTIONS

Within Europe, low-cost airlines such as EasyJet (www.easyjet.com) and Ryanair (www.ryanair.com) offer some highly attractive prices that can sometimes beat the cost of travelling by train. But the tickets are not always bargains; they are priced according to availability and demand. As always, it is usually best to book as far in advance as possible. Keep in mind that Ryanair flies in and out of Beauvais airport, 70km (43 miles) from Paris, so the low cost of a ticket may not be worth the time lost in travelling back and forth to the airport. EasyJet uses Roissy Charles de Gaulle airport.

EUROSTAR

The Eurostar (☎ 08705 186 186 from the UK; www.eurostar.com) takes you from London into the heart of Paris to the Gare du Nord in about 2 hours 15 minutes. From here there are good Métro and RER connections, or you can take a taxi.

Getting Around

TOURIST OFFICE

- Office du Tourisme de Paris 25 rue des Pyramides, 75001 08 92 68 30 00; www.parisinfo.com Jun–end Oct daily 9–7; Nov–end May daily 10–7 (Sun from 11) Pyramides English-speaking staff

VISITORS WITH DISABILITIES

Paris has a poor record on access and amenities. On the Métro, only the Meteor line (No. 14) has easy access for people with disabilities. Buses are similarly poorly equipped. RATP's Les Compagnons du Voyage (01 53 11 11 12) provides companions for visitors with disabilities (if not in an electric wheelchair), but for a fee. Taxi drivers are required to assist wheelchair users. The website of the Paris Tourist Office (www.parisinfo.com) has useful information for visitors with disabilities, including a list of accessible sights. Also try www.access-able.com.

MÉTRO

The best way to travel around Paris is by Métro or RER, two separate but linked systems. The RER is the suburban line, which passes through the heart of the city. The Métro is the underground system, with 14 lines and 372 stations. Both are inexpensive and efficient, and free maps of all the routes are available at station ticket windows. Any place is within easy walking distance of a Métro or RER station. Both systems function the same way and the tickets are interchangeable within the city. It is cheaper to buy a *carnet* of 10 tickets than to buy each ticket separately.

- Métro lines are identified by their destination and a number; connections are shown in *correspondances* panels on the platform.
- Blue *sortie* signs show the exits.
- The first Métros run at 5.30am, and the last around 12.45am (2.15am Fri and Sat).
- Keep your ticket until you exit—it has to be re-slotted on the RER, and ticket inspectors prowl the Métro.
- Try to avoid rush hours: 8–9.30am and 4.30–7pm.

TICKETS AND PASSES

- Tickets and passes function for Métro, buses and RER.
- One ticket (€1.60) gives access to the whole Métro network, the RER within Paris, Parisian

and suburban buses. A *carnet* of 10 tickets is €11.60.

- Prices of passes and suburban RER tickets depend on how many travel zones you intend to pass through.
- Mobilis is a one-day pass, valid on Métro, buses and RER.
- A Paris Visite card gives unlimited travel for one, two, three or five days plus discounts at certain monuments, but you need to do a lot of travelling to make it pay.
- The Carte Orange pass is being phased out in favour of the Navigo Smart Card for residents and Navigo Découverte for visitors. Photo ID is required for purchase.

BATOBUS

Travelling by Batobus—a river shuttle boat—is fun (mid-Mar to end May daily 10–7; Jun–end Aug 10–9.30; Sep–end Nov 10–7; Feb to mid-Mar 10.30– 4.30; closed most of Jan, Dec). It stops at the Eiffel Tower, Musée d'Orsay, Saint-Germain-des-Prés, Notre-Dame, Jardin des Plantes, Hôtel de Ville, Louvre and Champs-Élysées. You can join at any point. An all-day ticket costs €12 (☎ 0825 01 01 01; www.batobus.com).

TAXIS

Taxis can be hailed in the street if the roof sign is illuminated or can be found at most main attractions in taxi ranks. Sunday and night rates (7pm–7am) rise considerably and extra charges are made for station pickup and luggage. Taxi drivers expect tips of 10 per cent.

STUDENT VISITORS

- An International Student Identity Card can reduce cinema charges, entrance to museums and air and rail travel.
- MIJE (Maison Internationale de la Jeunesse et des Étudiants) ✉ 6 rue de Fourcy, 75004 ☎ 01 42 74 23 45; www.mije.com Ⓜ Saint-Paul ⏲ Daily 7am–1am. Three hostels for young people in the heart of Paris.
- CIDJ (Centre d'Information et de Documentation Jeunesse) ✉ 101 quai Branly, 75015 ☎ 01 44 49 12 00; www.cidj.com Ⓜ Bir-Hakeim ⏲ Mon, Wed, Fri 10–6, Tue, Thu 1–6, Sat 9.30–1). Youth information office for jobs, courses, sport.

TAXIS

- The initial fee for hiring a taxi is €2 and the rate in central Paris (Mon–Sat 7am–7pm) is €0.77 per km. From 7pm–7am and on Sundays and public holidays the rate increases to €1.09 per km. If luggage weighs more than 5kg there is an excess of €1.
- Taxi ranks that have phones can be called on ☎ 01 45 30 30 30. Select your *arrondissement* with the help of the voice server, who will then put you through to the closest rank.

Essential Facts

VISA AND TRAVEL INSURANCE

Visas are not required for EU, US or Canadian nationals, but you will need a valid passport. (Always check the latest requirements before you travel). EU citizens receive reduced-cost medical treatment with the European Health Insurance Card (EHIC). Full insurance is still strongly advised and is essential for all other travellers.

MONEY

The euro is the official currency of France. Bank notes in denominations of 5, 10, 20, 50, 100, 200 and 500 euros and coins in denominations of 1, 2, 5, 10, 20 and 50 cents and 1 and 2 euros were introduced on 1 January 2002.

10 euros

50 euros

200 euros

500 euros

CREDIT CARDS

- Credit cards are widely accepted.
- VISA cards are the most widely accepted and can be used in cash dispensers. Make sure you know your international PIN. MasterCard and Diners Club are also widely accepted.
- American Express is less common, so Amex cardholders needing cash should use American Express ✉ 11 rue Scribe, 75009 ☎ 01 47 77 70 00 Ⓜ Opéra.

ETIQUETTE

- Shake hands on introduction and on leaving; once you know people well replace this with a peck on both cheeks.
- Always use *vous* unless the other person breaks into *tu*.
- It is polite to add *Monsieur*, *Madame* or *Mademoiselle* when addressing strangers.
- Always say *bonjour* and *au revoir* in shops.
- When calling waiters, use *Monsieur* or *Madame* (not *garçon*).
- Dress carefully. More emphasis is put on grooming in France than in other countries.

FOREIGN EXCHANGE

- Only banks with Change signs change foreign currency/traveller's cheques; a passport is necessary. Bureaux de change are open longer hours but rates can be poorer. Rates for cashing euro traveller's cheques can be high.
- Airport and station exchange desks are open daily 6 or 6.30am to 10 or 10.30pm.

MEDICINES AND MEDICAL TREATMENT

- Minor ailments can often be treated at pharmacies (identified by a green cross).
- All public hospitals have a 24-hour emergency service (*urgences*) as well as specialist doctors. Payment is made on the spot, but if you are hospitalized see the *assistante sociale* to arrange payment through your insurance.
- House calls are made by SOS Médecins. ☎ 01 47 07 77 77 or 0820 33 24 24; for dental problems SOS Dentaire ☎ 01 43 37 51 00.

• 24-hour pharmacy: Les Champs ✉ 84 avenue des Champs-Élysées, 75008 ☎ 01 45 62 02 41.
• Publicis drugstore at 133 avenue des Champs-Élysées (☎ 01 44 43 79 00) offers pharmacies, cafés, newsagents and tobacconists, open until 2am.

NATIONAL HOLIDAYS

• 1 January, Easter Monday, 1 May, 8 May, Ascension (a Thursday in May), Whit Monday (late May or early June), 14 July, 15 August, 1 November, 11 November, 25 December.
• Sunday services for public transport operate; many local shops, restaurants and even large stores disregard national holidays.

POST OFFICES

• Stamps can be bought at *tabacs*; post mail in any yellow mailbox.
• All post offices offer express courier post (Chronopost), and photocopy machines.

EMERGENCY NUMBERS

• Crisis-line in English: SOS Help ☎ 01 46 21 46 46 🕐 3pm–11pm
• Police ☎ 17
• Any emergency ☎ 112
• Ambulance (SAMU) ☎ 15
• Fire (*sapeurs pompiers*) ☎ 18
• Anti-poison ☎ 01 40 05 48 48
• Police lost-property office is ✉ 36 rue des Morillons, 75015 ☎ 08 21 00 25 25

ELECTRICITY

• Voltage is 220V; French sockets take plugs with two round pins.

PLACES OF WORSHIP

Protestant churches	American Church ✉ 65 quai d'Orsay, 75007 ☎ 01 40 62 05 00 Ⓜ Invalides
	Saint George's English Church ✉ 7 rue Auguste Vacquerie, 75016 ☎ 01 47 20 22 51 Ⓜ Charles de Gaulle–Étoile, Kleber
	The Scots Kirk ✉ 17 rue Bayard, 75008 ☎ 01 48 78 47 94 Ⓜ F D Roosevelt, Champs-Élysées–Clemenceau
Jewish	Synagogue ✉ 10 rue Pavée, 75004 ☎ 01 42 77 81 51 Ⓜ St-Paul
Muslim	Grande Mosquée de Paris ✉ 2 bis place du Puits-de-l'Ermite, 75005 ☎ 01 45 35 97 33 Ⓜ Place Monge

For Catholic churches, see the individual entries in the Paris by Area section of this book. The Tourist Office has details of other places of worship.

EMBASSIES/CONSULATES

British Embassy	✉ 35 rue du Faubourg Saint-Honoré, 75008 ☎ 01 44 51 31 00
British Consulate	✉ 16 rue d'Anjou, 75008 ☎ 01 44 51 31 01/2
US Embassy	✉ 2 avenue Gabriel, 75008 ☎ 01 43 12 22 22
US Consulate	✉ 4 avenue Gabriel, 75008 ☎ 01 43 12 22 22
Canadian Embassy	✉ 35 avenue Montaigne, 75008 ☎ 01 44 43 29 00
Australian Embassy	✉ 4 rue Jean-Rey, 75015 ☎ 01 40 59 33 00
New Zealand Embassy	✉ 7ter rue Léonard-de-Vinci, 75016 ☎ 01 45 01 43 43

OPENING HOURS

- Banks: Mon–Fri 9–12.30, 2–4. Closed on public holidays and often the preceding afternoon.
- Post offices: Mon–Fri 8–7, Sat 8–12. The main post office (✉ 52 rue du Louvre, 75001) provides a 24-hour service for post, telegrams and telephone.
- Shops: Mon–Sat 9–7 or 10–8. Some close Mon and an hour at lunch.
- Museums: national museums close on Tue, municipal museums on Mon. Individual opening hours vary.

PRESS

- Main dailies are *Le Monde* (serious, centrist), *Libération* (left-wing) and *Le Figaro* (right-wing).
- For weekly listings of cultural events, buy a copy of *Pariscope* (the most popular listings magazine) or *L'Officiel des Spectacles*.
- Central newspaper kiosks and newsagents stock European dailies (widely available on the day of issue) and *USA Today*.
- Visit www.trouverlapress.com to find out exactly where you can buy your favourite publication.

SENSIBLE PRECAUTIONS

- Watch wallets and handbags as pickpockets are active, particularly in busy bars, flea markets, cinemas, Métro and rail stations and the airport.
- Keep traveller's-cheque numbers separate from the cheques.
- It is important to make a declaration at a local *commissariat* (police station) to claim losses on your insurance.
- Women are generally safe travelling alone or together, although the same risks apply as in any city in western Europe. Deal with any unwanted attention firmly and politely. Avoid the Métro late at night.

TELEPHONES

- Most phone booths use France Telecom cards (*télécarte* for 25, 50 or 120 units), sold at post offices, *tabacs* or main Métro stations.
- Information ☎ 118 712
- International information ☎ 118 700
- To call France from the UK dial 00 33—omit the first zero from the number. To call the UK from France, dial 00 44—omit the first zero.
- To call France from the US dial 011 33, then leave out the first zero. To call the US from France dial 00 1 followed by the number.
- All numbers in the Île-de-France, including Paris, start with 01 unless at extra rates, when they start with 08; some are toll-free.
- Numbers in the French provinces begin with: 02 Northwest, 03 Northeast, 04 Southeast, 05 Southwest.

TICKETS

- The Paris Museum Pass (www.parismuseumpass.com) gives access to 60 museums. It is valid for 2, 4 or 6 days. You can buy it online or at tourist offices, museums and Fnac shops.

TOILETS

- Public toilet booths are common, free and are generally well maintained.
- Every café has a toilet (ask for *'Les toilettes, s'il vous plaît?'*), but order a drink first.

Language

BASIC VOCABULARY	
oui/non	yes/no
s'il vous plaît	please
merci	thank you
excusez-moi	excuse me
bonjour	hello
bonsoir	good evening
au revoir	good-bye
parlez-vous anglais?	do you speak English?
je ne comprends pas	I don't understand
combien?	how much?
où est/sont...?	where is/are ...?
ici/là	here/there
tournez à gauche/droite	turn left/right
tout droit	straight on
quand?	when?
aujourd'hui	today
hier	yesterday
demain	tomorrow
combien de temps?	how long?
à quelle heure?	at what time?
à quelle heure ouvrez/fermez-vous?	what time do you open/close?
avez-vous...?	do you have ...?
une chambre simple	a single room
une chambre double	a double room
avec/sans salle de bains	with/without bathroom
le petit déjeuner	breakfast
le déjeuner	lunch
le dîner	dinner
c'est combien?	how much is this?
acceptez-vous des cartes de credit?	do you take credit cards?
j'ai besoin d'un médecin/dentiste	I need a doctor/dentist
pouvez-vous m'aider?	can you help me?
où est l'hôpital?	where is the hospital?
où est le commissariat?	where is the police station?

NUMBERS	
un	1
deux	2
trois	3
quatre	4
cinq	5
six	6
sept	7
huit	8
neuf	9
dix	10
onze	11
douze	12
treize	13
quatorze	14
quinze	15
seize	16
dix-sept	17
dix-huit	18
dix-neuf	19
vingt	20
vingt-et-un	21
trente	30
quarante	40
cinquante	50
soixante	60
soixante-dix	70
quatre-vingts	80
quatre-vingt-dix	90
cent	100
mille	1,000

Timeline

BEFORE 1000

Celtic tribe of Parisii settles on Île de la Cité around 200BC.

By AD100 the Roman city of Lutetia, later Paris, is growing fast.

In 451 Saint Geneviève saves Paris from the threat of Attila the Hun.

REIGN OF TERROR

From 1793 to 1794 the Reign of Terror seized France, masterminded by the ruthless, power-crazed Jacobin leaders Robespierre and Danton. The king, Louis XVI, was convicted of treason and guillotined in January 1793, followed in October by his queen, Marie-Antoinette. By mid-1794 more than 18,000 people are estimated to have been beheaded in France.

1163 The building of Notre-Dame starts.

1337–1453 Hundred Years War between France and England.

1431 Henry VI of England is crowned king of France in Notre-Dame.

1437 Charles VII regains control of Paris.

1572 St. Bartholomew Massacre occurs during Wars of Religion.

1682 Louis XIV and the court move to Versailles.

1700s Intellectuals introduce radical new ideas during the Age of Enlightment.

1789 Storming of the Bastille.

1792 Monarchy abolished; proclamation of the Republic.

1804 Napoleon crowned emperor.

1830 Bourbons overthrown; Louis-Philippe crowned.

1848 Revolution topples Louis-Philippe; Second Republic headed by Napoleon III, later crowned emperor.

1852–70 Baron Haussmann oversees the transformation of Paris.

1870–71 Paris besieged by Prussians, civil uprising of the Commune, Republic restored.

1889 Eiffel Tower is completed.

1900 First Métro line opens.

1914–18 Paris bombarded by German cannon, Big Bertha.

1940 Nazis occupy Paris, followed by Liberation in 1944.

1958 De Gaulle heads Fifth Republic.

1977 Jacques Chirac is elected mayor (he becomes president in 1995). Centre Georges Pompidou opens.

1981 Election of President Mitterrand. He initiates his Grands Projets–a scheme of new building projects.

1999 December storms hit Paris; Versailles loses more than 10,000 trees.

2002 Euro notes and coins are introduced.

2007 Nicolas Sarkozy is elected president. Paris hosts the Rugby World Cup final, won by South Africa.

2010 A new gallery for the Louvre's Islamic Arts department is installed in the Cour Visconti.

THE SEINE

The city's history has been inextricably linked with the Seine since its earliest origins as a Gaulish village on the Île de la Cité, an islet in the river. The river represents the very lifeblood of Paris, flowing through its heart, animating the city, defining the capital geographically and reflecting its history in its many fine buildings. After centuries of pollution–when the river was used as a sewer–the Seine has been cleaned and its water is less polluted than it has been for years, although Jacques Chirac never swam in it as he promised he would before the end of his presidency.

From left to right: Notre-Dame cathedral; Marie-Antoinette; an engraving showing the Bastille; detail of a tapestry from Flanders showing the crowning of Charles VII with Joan of Arc watching; the entry of Charlemagne

Index

INDEX

CITYPACK TOP 25
Paris

WRITTEN BY Fiona Dunlop
ADDITIONAL WRITING Heidi Ellison
UPDATED BY Adele Evans
COVER DESIGN AND DESIGN WORK Jacqueline Bailey
INDEXER Marie Lorimer
IMAGE RETOUCHING AND REPRO Sarah Montgomery and James Tims
PROJECT EDITOR Kathryn Glendenning
SERIES EDITOR Marie-Claire Jefferies

First published 1997
New edition 2007
Reprinted Sep 2007
Information verified and updated for 2011

Colour separation by AA Digital Department
Printed and bound by Leo Paper Products, China

A CIP catalogue record for this book is available from the British Library.

ISBN 978-0-7495-5092-9

Published by AA Publishing, a trading name of AA Media Limited, whose registered office is Fanum House, Basing View, Basingstoke, Hampshire RG21 4EA. Registered number 06112600.

A04202
Maps in this title produced from map data © Tele Atlas N.V. 2010 Tele Atlas
IGN France.
Transport map © Communicarta Ltd, UK

The Automobile Association would like to thank the following photographers, companies and picture libraries for their assistance in the preparation of this book.

Abbreviations for the picture credits are as follows: (t) top; (b) bottom; (l) left; (r) right; (AA) AA World Travel Library.

Front cover AA/M Jourdan; **back cover (i)** AA/W Voysey; **(ii)** AA/C Sawyer; **(iii)** AA/K Blackwell; **(iv)** AA/P Enticknap; **1** AA; **2** AA/B Rieger; **3** AA/B Rieger; **4t** AA/B Rieger; **4l** AA/K Paterson; **5t** AA/B Rieger; **5** AA/P Enticknap; **6t** AA/B Rieger; **6cl** AA/M Jourdan; **6c** AA/C Sawyer; **6cr** AA/A Souter; **6bl** AA/C Sawyer; **6br** AA/J A Tims; **7t** AA/B Rieger; **7cl** AA/M Jourdan; **7c** AA/M Jourdan; **7cr** AA/M Jourdan; **7bl** AA/J A Tims; **7br** AA/T Souter; **8t** AA/B Rieger; **9t** AA/B Rieger; **10t** AA/B Rieger; **10tr** AA/M Jourdan; **10c** AA/C Sawyer; **10b** AA/C Sawyer; **11tl** AA/C Sawyer; **11c** AA/C Sawyer; **11b** AA/C Sawyer; **10/11b** AA/M Jourdan; **12t** AA/B Rieger; **12t** AA/M Chaplow; **13t** AA/B Rieger; **13tl** AA/M Jourdan; **13ct** Brand X Pictures; **13c** AA/B Rieger; **13cb** AA/B Rieger; **13b** AA/M Jourdan; **14t** AA/B Rieger; **14tr** AA/C Sawyer; **14ct** AA/B Rieger; **14cb** AA/C Sawyer; **14b** AA/P Kenward; **15t** AA/B Rieger; **15b** AA/C Sawyer; **16t** AA/B Rieger; **16tr** AA/C Sawyer; **16cr** AA/C Sawyer; **16br** AA/C Sawyer; **17t** AA/B Rieger; **17tl** AA/M Jourdan; **17ctl** AA/J A Tims; **17cbl** AA/M Jourdan; **17bl** AA/M Jourdan; **18t** AA/B Rieger; **18tr** AA/C Sawyer; **18ctr** AA/M Jourdan; **18cbr** AA/M Jourdan; **18br** AA/C Sawyer; **19t** AA/K Paterson; **19ct** AA/P Enticknap; **19c** AA/M Jourdan; **19cb** AA/M Jourdan; **19bt** AA/C Sawyer; **19b** AA/M Jourdan; **20/1** AA/K Paterson; **24/5t** AA/K Paterson; **24c** AA/B Rieger; **24/5c** AA/K Paterson; **25** AA; **26l** AA/P Enticknap; **26/7** AA/M Jourdan; **26c** AA/M Jourdan; **27r** AA/C Sawyer; **27c** AA/T Souter; **27cl** AA/M Jourdan; **28l** AA/K Blackwell; **28r** AA/K Blackwell; **29l** AA/B Rieger; **29r** AA/K Paterson; **30/1t** AA/J A Tims; **30l** AA/B Rieger; **30c** AA/M Jourdan; **30/1c** AA/M Jourdan; **31** AA/T Souter; **32t** AA/C Sawyer; **32bl** AA/M Jourdan; **32br** AA/J A Tims; **33t** AA/C Sawyer; **33bl** AA/C Sawyer; **33bc** AA/M Jourdan; **33br** AA/M Jourdan; **34t** AA/C Sawyer; **34c** Digitalvision; **35** AA/C Sawyer; **36t** AA/C Sawyer; **37** AA/C Sawyer; **40** AA/T Souter; **40/1** AA/T Souter; **42l** AA/M Jourdan; **42r** AA/T Souter; **43l** AA/M Jourdan; **43r** AA/K Paterson; **44tl** AA/B Rieger; **44cl** AA/K Paterson; **44/5** AA/T Souter; **44cr** AA/C Sawyer; **45cl** AA/C Sawyer; **45r** AA/C Sawyer; **46l** AA/M Jourdan; **46/7t** AA/J A Tims; **46/7c** AA/K Paterson; **47tr** AA/M Jourdan; **47cr** AA/J A Tims; **48l** AA/K Paterson; **48r** AA/K Paterson; **49** AA/C Sawyer; **50t** AA/C Sawyer; **50bl** AA/M Jourdan; **50br** AA/M Jourdan; **51t** AA/C Sawyer; **51b** AA/M Jourdan; **52t** AA/C Sawyer; **52c** AA/K Blackwell; **52b** AA/C Sawyer; **53** AA/M Jourdan; **54t** AA/C Sawyer; **55t** Digitalvision; **56t** AA/C Sawyer; **57** AA/C Sawyer; **60tl** AA/C Sawyer; **60/1t** AA/M Jourdan; **60cl** AA/C Sawyer; **60/1c** AA/M Jourdan; **61** AA/T Souter; **62l** AA/M Jourdan; **62r** AA/M Jourdan; **63l** AA/K Paterson; **63r** AA/B Rieger; **64t** AA/C Sawyer; **64bl** AA/B Rieger; **64br** AA/J A Tims; **65t** AA/C Sawyer; **65bl** AA/M Jourdan; **65br** AA/K Paterson; **66t** AA/M Jourdan; **67** AA/M Jourdan; **68t** AA/C Sawyer; **69t** AA; **70t** AA/C Sawyer; **71** AA/M Jourdan; **74l** AA/M Jourdan; **74c** AA/M Jourdan; **74r** AA/T Souter; **75l** AA/M Jourdan; **75r** AA; **76l** AA/M Jourdan; **76/7t** AA/J A Tims; **76c** AA/J A Tims; **76/7c** AA/J A Tims; **77** AA/P Enticknap; **78l** AA/M Jourdan; **78r** AA/K Paterson; **79** AA/K Blackwell; **80l** AA/M Jourdan; **80r** AA/B Rieger; **81t** AA/C Sawyer; **81b** AA/J A Tims; **82t** AA/C Sawyer; **82bl** AA/K Paterson; **82br** AA/M Jourdan; **83t** AA/M Jourdan; **84t** AA/C Sawyer; **85t** AA/M Jourdan; **86t** AA/C Sawyer; **87** AA/K Paterson; **90tl** AA/K Paterson; **90cl** AA/K Paterson; **90/1t** AA/J A Tims; **90/1c** AA/J A Tims; **91** AA/T Souter; **92t** AA/C Sawyer; **92bl** AA/P Kenward; **92br** AA/C Sawyer; **93t** AA/M Jourdan; **94t** AA/C Sawyer; **95t** AA/T Souter; **96t** AA/T Souter; **97** AA/C Sawyer; **100l** AA/W Voysey; **100r** AA/C Sawyer; **101l** AA/C Sawyer; **101r** AA/J A Tims; **102t** AA/J A Tims; **102r** AA/M Jourdan; **103l** AA/M Jourdan; **103r** AA/D Noble; **104t** AA/C Sawyer; **104bl** AA/T Souter; **104br** AA/M Jourdan; **105t** AA/D Noble; **105bl** AA/K Paterson; **105bc** AA/D Noble; **105br** AA/D Noble; **106t** AA/C Sawyer; **107** AA/C Sawyer; **108t** AA/C Sawyer; **108tr** AA/C Sawyer; **108tcr** AA/C Sawyer; **108bcr** AA/C Sawyer; **108cr** AA/S McBride; **109t** AA/C Sawyer; **110t** AA/C Sawyer; **111t** AA/C Sawyer; **112t** AA/C Sawyer; **113** AA/C Sawyer; **114t** AA/M Jourdan; **115t** AA/M Jourdan; **116t** AA/M Jourdan; **116b** AA/C Sawyer; **117t** AA/M Jourdan; **117r** AA/C Sawyer; **117b** AA/C Sawyer; **118t** AA/M Jourdan; **118c** AA/C Sawyer; **119t** AA/M Jourdan; **119l** AA/T Souter; **120t** AA/M Jourdan; **120b** European Central Bank; **121t** AA/M Jourdan; **121r** AA/C Sawyer; **122t** AA/M Jourdan; **123t** AA/M Jourdan; **123b** AA/M Jourdan; **124t** AA/M Jourdan; **124bl** AA/P Enticknap; **124bc** AA; **124br** AA; **125t** AA/M Jourdan; **125bl** AA/R Moore; **125br** AA.

Every effort has been made to trace the copyright holders, and we apologise in advance for any accidental errors. We would be happy to apply the corrections in the following edition of this publication.